IGNITE YOUR SPARK

DISCOVERING WHO YOU ARE FROM THE INSIDE OUT

PATRICIA WOOSTER

Simon Pulse
New York London Toronto Sydney New Delhi

 BEYOND WORDS
Hillsboro, Oregon

An Imprint of Simon & Schuster, Inc.
Children's Publishing Division
1230 Avenue of the Americas
New York, NY 10020
1230 Avenue of the Americas
New York, NY 10020

20827 N.W. Cornell Road, Suite 500
Hillsboro, Oregon 97124-9808
503-531-8700 / 503-531-8773 fax
www.beyondword.com
503-531-8700 / 503-531-8773 fax
www.beyondword.com

This Beyond Words/Simon Pulse edition January 2017
Text copyright © 2017 by Patricia Wooster
Cover copyright © 2017 by Beyond Words/Simon & Schuster, Inc.

Managing Editor: Lindsay S. Easterbrooks-Brown
Editor: Emmalisa Sparrow
Copyeditor: Ali Shaw
Proofreader: Ashley Van Winkle
Cover design: Sara E. Blum
Interior design: Devon Smith
Composition: William H. Brunson Typography Services
The text of this book was set in Minion Pro.

For information about special discounts for bulk purchases, please contact Simon & Schuster
Special Sales at 1-866-506-1949 or business@simonandschuster.com.

The Simon & Schuster Speakers Bureau can bring authors to your live event. For more
information or to book an event contact the Simon & Schuster Speakers Bureau at
1-866-248-3049 or visit our website at www.simonspeakers.com.

Manufactured in the United States of America

10 9 8 7 6 5 4 3 2 1

Library of Congress Cataloging-in-Publication Data

Names: Wooster, Patricia, author.
Title: Ignite your spark : discovering who you are from the inside out /
   Patricia Wooster.
Description: New York ; Hillsboro, Oregon : Simon Pulse/Beyond Words, 2017. |
   Includes bibliographical references and index.
Identifiers: LCCN 2016018821 (print) | LCCN 2016029879 (ebook) |
   ISBN 9781582705651 (hardcover : alk. paper) | ISBN 9781582705644
   (pbk. : alk. paper) | ISBN 9781481443661 (eBook)
Subjects: LCSH: Self-perception in adolescence—Juvenile literature. |
   Self-realization—Juvenile literature. | Self-actualization (Psychology)
   in adolescence—Juvenile literature.
Classification: LCC BF724.3.S35 W66 2017 (print) | LCC BF724.3.S35 (ebook) |
   DDC 155.5/19—dc23
LC record available at https://lccn.loc.gov/2016018821

FOR MY HUSBAND, SCOT, AND SONS, MAX AND JACK—
MAY YOU IGNITE YOUR SPARK EVERY SINGLE DAY.

CONTENTS

AUTHOR'S NOTE

If you walked into my office right now, what would you see? You'd see piles upon piles of articles and books on ordinary youth doing extraordinary things. I have newspaper clippings and internet printouts tacked onto bulletin boards. On my whiteboard, I have an ever-changing list of kids and teens I want to interview. This sits next to a bookshelf full of nonfiction and fiction books—and even memoirs—written by people who still have to get up and go to school in the morning.

This collection of youth success stories started in 2012 when I was asked to write a book called *So, You Want to Work in Fashion?* for teens who were interested in fashion design. Part of my job was to interview young adults already working in the industry. Next came a book in the same series about leadership, where I found an equal number of successful young adults. They were even more impressive during their interviews than they were on paper.

The question that kept coming back to me was, How are these ordinary teens doing such extraordinary things? Do they have access to better education? More supportive parents? Are they geniuses? Trust fund babies? Or related to celebrities?

I decided I wanted answers to these questions. In the process, I got to talk to some of the most inspirational, interesting, and unique people I've ever encountered. What I found to be the common thread among these super-amazing young adults was that their foundation of success was built with a strong sense of self-identity, determination, and grit. This book is my opportunity to share my research and teach others how they can incorporate these skills into their daily lives. I hope it inspires you to ignite your own spark!

Throughout the book you'll see these two symbols:

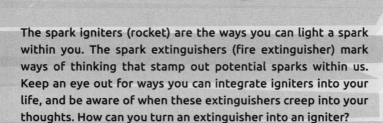

The spark igniters (rocket) are the ways you can light a spark within you. The spark extinguishers (fire extinguisher) mark ways of thinking that stamp out potential sparks within us. Keep an eye out for ways you can integrate igniters into your life, and be aware of when these extinguishers creep into your thoughts. How can you turn an extinguisher into an igniter?

1

WHAT IS YOUR SPARK?

Ignite: to give life or energy to; to set (something) on fire
—Merriam-Webster Dictionary

Wouldn't it be great if you woke up every morning excited and energized because your days were filled with a purpose? Or if you looked in the mirror and liked the person staring back at you? What if you could improve your relationships and spend time with people who share and support your interests? Your spark includes the best parts of yourself that you can use to fulfill your dreams, love who you are, and take your life in the direction that makes you the most happy. That's what igniting your spark is all about: discovering and becoming the person you want to be.

You don't have to be an adult or out of school to start boosting your self-identity. You can do it right now.

Your spark is not what your parents want you to do, or what will look good on your school transcripts, or even about what your friends are doing. Igniting your spark is about connecting you to the things that make you want to jump out of bed in the morning. All you need is curiosity and the willingness to try something new. Whether you are interested in finding a new hobby, making new friends, or feeling better about how you look—you are in control of your life's direction.

Start looking for opportunities to make positive changes in your life—we'll discuss the whens, whys, and hows in this book—and get ready to remove any barriers standing in your way. This is your journey!

ANYWHERE HIGH SCHOOL

Morgan and Drew are best friends and total opposites. Morgan doesn't mind standing out from the crowd with her hair dyed a different color every week; Drew likes to blend in and go unnoticed. While Morgan finds a way to do the activities she likes, Drew never quite gets around to pursuing a hobby. He's afraid of missing out on a social activity if he commits to something new.

"I can't hang out with you tonight. I've got that race tomorrow morning with my dad, and then I've got band practice," Morgan says.

"You have to go to Jackson's party with me," Drew says into the phone. "I can't walk in there alone."

"Why would you even consider going? He's a jerk to you most of the time," Morgan says. "Why don't you do something fun instead?"

"If I miss the party, Jackson will probably talk crap about me."

"What a great friend," Morgan says sarcastically. "You should try hanging out with somebody else."

"That's easy for you to say," Drew says. "You've got your bandmates and running pals to hang out with."

"You could start drawing again. There's some pretty cool kids who get together at Murphy's Coffee Shop on Friday nights to draw anime," Morgan says. "You should check it out."

"I've thought about it, but something always comes up. I'm afraid if I stop showing up to parties I'll no longer be invited."

DOING IT THE HARD WAY

A lot has changed since I was in school, but the basic issues have stayed the same—expectations from parents, insecurities, peer pressure, school cliques, and so on. My greatest wishes were to fit in, have some sort of talent, and feel good about how I looked. I spent so much time trying to blend in that I forgot who I really was, and I stopped asking myself what I wanted out of life.

I always loved to write. It started with poems and stories no one would ever see. In class I doodled and wrote ideas in the margins of my notebooks. At home I pretended to do my homework while documenting my entire day in my journal. I wrote about problems with friends, my insecurities, and dreams for my future. And then life got in the way and I stopped writing.

After college I didn't even consider looking for a job where I could write. I was living in Kansas and thought to be a writer you had to be living in New York City working for a magazine publisher. I didn't know how many different companies utilize writers for things like: marketing, technical documents, employee manuals, or website content. The expectations were for me to go out and find a job where I could earn enough money to be self-sufficient. No one told me I could earn a living doing something I actually enjoyed. I went out and got your basic entry-level job and spent all of my free time with friends. I suffered from major FOMO (fear of missing out), so I never missed a party or outing. It took many years, several jobs, and having a couple of kids for me to realize how much I missed putting pen to paper.

So, I started writing. And then I found a local writing group, which introduced me to new writing techniques. And I noticed how great it made me feel, which caused me to start believing in myself, and I started developing friendships with other writers, who helped me find opportunities to publish, which made me excited to sit down and write every day. And my life made a radical shift, and my spark was ignited.

REASONS TO LIGHT THAT SPARK

Don't let time take you farther away from what you like to do. It took me more than twenty years to get back to my passion. You're never too young to create your own identity and pursue your dreams. Once you embrace who you are, all kinds of doors will start to open for you. Things will begin to fall into place. When I started doing what I loved, new opportunities began to present themselves to me. Once I put the word out "this is who I am," people began to approach me about projects, or introduce me to others with the same passion. It will happen for you too. All you need to do is take the first step. Here are a few suggestions to get you started.

Have Fun

Stop wasting time doing things you don't enjoy. If you don't like sports, don't try out for the basketball team. Sign up for an art class instead. This is your time to try all kinds of new things. There are no right or wrong activities if you're doing something you enjoy. Don't be afraid to look outside of your school's offerings during your search. Who knows? Your new hobby may lead you toward your future career.

Love Who You Are

Doing something without passion. *I don't really care what I do as long as I'm good at it.*

Look in the mirror and love what you see. Stop obsessing over your flaws. Very few people look like supermodels or professional athletes. Enhancing your best features and embracing your uniqueness can be a lot of fun. You may have to experiment with different clothing styles and how you want to present yourself, but you'll feel great when your outside appearance matches the type of person you are on the inside.

Find Great Friends

Once you know who you are and feel good
about yourself, you'll start seeking out
people who support your dreams. Your
friendships will improve. Communication
at home will get better. You'll find yourself gravitating to people who have similar

Create your own inner
fandom. *I like who I am.*

interests and beliefs. Think how great it would feel to not worry about
what other people think. True friends will love and respect you for who
you are.

As you travel through this book, you will discover all sorts of paths you
can take toward forming your own identity. Various experts will offer
you their advice. You will take self-discovery quizzes and be given explor-
atory exercises. This will help you assess who you are and identify who
you want to be. You will read interviews from people of all ages doing
amazing things. You'll hear from a magician, a gymnast, an entrepreneur,
a writer, and many more. They have very different dreams, but they all
share a similar message. Knowing who they are and loving what they do
has changed their lives. It can change your life too.

Spark Quiz
What's Confidence Got to Do with It?

Everyone needs a healthy dose of self-confidence to pursue
their dreams. You need to be open to making changes and taking risks in order to discover who you are. If you feel good about

yourself, you'll have an easier time making friends, handling problems, and avoiding peer pressure. If you feel bad about yourself, it's easy to become critical and to make bad decisions. Before you can ignite your spark, you need to think about what's holding you back. Here's a short quiz to get you thinking. Answer *true* or *false* for each of the following questions.

1. I would rather be myself than change who I am to fit in.
   True or False
2. I set goals for myself and then set out to achieve them.
   True or False
3. When I look in the mirror, I like what I see.
   True or False
4. I have no problem standing up for what I believe in.
   True or False
5. I'm my biggest cheerleader.
   True or False
6. I'm comfortable around new people.
   True or False
7. I try new activities even if my friends don't participate.
   True or False
8. I can get lost in an activity I enjoy.
   True or False
9. I know how to ask for help when needed.
   True or False
10. I don't need to be the center of attention.
    True or False

Congratulate yourself for every time you answered *true*! This means you are confident in this area. If you answered *false* for any question, that's okay. We will be working on these areas throughout the book. Some of these changes will be easy to make, and others will take some time. Feel free to come back to this quiz at any time. It's a great way to check your level of confidence.

Illuminator: Aly Raisman, Olympic Gymnast

If you didn't catch Aly Raisman igniting her dreams during the 2012 Summer Olympics or on *Dancing with the Stars* in 2013, then maybe you saw her once again lighting up the gymnastics floor at the 2016 Olympic Games in Rio, Brazil. In both 2012 and 2016, she was the captain of the women's gold medal–winning gymnastics teams. In 2012, she took home a gold medal for floor exercises and a bronze medal for balance beam. In 2016, she earned an individual silver medal for the women's all-around. She's a great example of someone who uses grit, determination, and hard work to pursue her love of gymnastics. Read on to learn how this five-time Olympic medalist found her passion.

1. How did you discover gymnastics was your true passion?
I started gymnastics when I was two, so it's all I've ever known. I was very active when I was younger and always doing so many sports like baseball, soccer, ice-skating, and basketball, but gymnastics was always my favorite.

2. What do you love most about the sport and being part of a team?
I love how gymnastics never gets boring and there is always something that needs more work. My favorite thing about being a part of a

team is the bond that I form with my teammates. There is nothing like having great friends.

3. How do you keep a positive attitude when things aren't going your way?

Having a positive attitude and confidence is such a crucial part of anything that you do in life. Even if things aren't going my way and I feel tired or frustrated, I try to remember I'm human and no one is perfect. The bad days are what make us stronger. If I'm nervous to compete, what keeps me going is the image of competing well and believing in myself. Hard work always turns into confidence.

4. Where do you think your confidence comes from?

My confidence comes from the hard work I put into gymnastics. I work every day, and I try to do a lot of numbers and repetitions so by the time I compete, I feel confident and ready. I don't ever want to look back and have regrets or wish I'd worked harder. I think that would be the worst feeling in the world. I've never felt that way, and I never want to.

5. After so much hard work, how did it feel to win three medals at the 2012 Summer Olympics?

I felt very relieved and happy to have won three medals. The whole year leading up to the Olympics, I was stressed and felt a lot of pressure because I'd dreamed of the Olympics since I was eight years old and my chance had finally come. I was proud and honored to have done so well for not only my country, but also for my family and coaches who'd been supporting me every step of the way.

6. What advice can you give teens about pursuing their dreams?

Always set high goals for yourself and believe you can do it. I always feel believing is half the battle. It is definitely easier said than done!

7. Where do you see yourself in ten years?
I'm not really sure. I guess married with kids. I'll be almost thirty then. I'll always be involved in the sport of gymnastics. I know that much.

8. What's something most of your fans don't know about you?
I love singing in the car on the way to practice. Singing to my favorite songs makes me feel calm and relaxed before a long, hard workout.

THE COMPARISON TRAP

I'm sure you've been told not to compare yourself to other people. This is good advice, but it also falls under the easier-said-than-done category. It's difficult not to wonder... Who's better looking? Who's smarter? Who has the most friends? Who's better at sports? It's easy to start picking out your own flaws while discounting your assets.

Be unique. *I don't need to be like everyone else.*

And what about the people on social media? They seem to have it all together. You can read about their dates, college acceptance letters, and the great parties they attend on weekends. They post selfies and videos, and they always seem to be having a great time. What they don't tell you is about their insecurities, or the not-so-great things happening in their lives. Keep this in mind when you're on the internet. People on social media only show you the things they want you to see, which is mostly just the good stuff.

Being your own biggest bully. *I am such a loser!*

The comparison game is where you can trip yourself up. You might wonder why you aren't part of the *in* crowd at school.

You may want to be just like them. You may copy their clothes, join their activities, and start acting like them. This may go against how you like to dress and what you like to do, but you do it to fit in. Masking your true identity robs everyone (including yourself) of the opportunity to get to know the real you. Challenge yourself to be proud of who you are as an individual. Trust me—you'll be much happier representing your true self.

CELEBRITIES WHO CONSIDERED THEMSELVES AWKWARD AS TEENS

Do you think you need to be like everyone else? Guess what—you don't. Each one of you has your own individual personality and talents for a reason. Here are a few celebrities who describe themselves as awkward teens but stayed true to themselves and weren't afraid to follow their dreams.

* Brittany Snow
* Chad Michael Murray
* Charlize Theron
* Chris Colfer
* Hugh Jackman
* Jennifer Garner
* Jessica Alba
* J. K. Rowling
* Kristen Stewart
* Malin Akerman
* Naya Rivera
* Rihanna
* Ryan Reynolds
* Selena Gomez
* Taylor Swift

Illuminator: Jack Andraka, Author of *Breakthrough: How One Teen Innovator Is Changing the World*

What do you do when a close family friend dies from one of the most lethal types of cancer? If you are Jack Andraka, you do a ton of research and when you turn fifteen years old, you invent an early detection test for pancreatic, lung, and ovarian cancers. He won the Smithsonian American Ingenuity Youth Achievement Award (2012), the Jefferson Award (2014), and the Siemens Foundation We Can Change the World High School Challenge (2014) for this invention. He is a public speaker and has been featured in several documentaries. A National Geographic Emerging Explorer grant has provided the funding for him to work on a nanorobot and a cancer-fighting drug-delivery system while still improving his pancreatic cancer test. In 2015 he published his first book, titled *Breakthrough: How One Teen Innovator Is Changing the World*, an inspirational memoir including science experiments you can try at home or in the classroom. Jack never stopped looking for his niche. He kept trying new activities until he found his passion. To read more about Jack and his research visit him at jackandraka.com. Read on to learn how he has let nothing stand in the way of his success.

1. Tell me about your high school years.
My middle school years were really formative for my experiences in high school. I hadn't fit in well in elementary school—it was more focused on the arts than math and science, so it was a big relief to go to a math and science charter school. I was able to learn and practice and improve not only my science and math skills but also my presentation skills—which are very important for scientists, because if people aren't engaged with or can't understand your work, then it won't make much of a difference. As Einstein said, "If you can't explain it simply, you don't understand it well enough." I was fortunate enough to win the Intel International Science and Engineering Fair my freshman year. It was a surreal and

overwhelming experience for me (the video of me winning went viral) that helped give me a platform to raise awareness of problems I was facing—big problems like the need for more funding for research for pancreatic cancer; the need for open access to scientific journal articles so that people, no matter what their gender, race, or socioeconomic status, could have access to knowledge locked away behind these paywalls; and the importance of recognizing the LGBT community is made up of not only fashion designers but also computer scientists, mathematicians, and scientists.

I missed a lot of school the next few years, traveling around the world to speak about these issues, and also spent a lot of time in the lab working on improving my pancreatic sensor and thinking of other sensors and their applications. I did carve out some time to compete for a spin on the US Wildwater kayak team—I grew up kayaking on whitewater rivers and was so happy to make the team my freshman year. Although I wasn't able to continue my training because my schedule got so busy, I still spent time hopping in my kayak for river trips to West Virginia or Pennsylvania with my family and came back with a clearer mind and sore muscles.

I made sure to enjoy senior year. I joined the varsity swim team and got to feel the sense of camaraderie and competition I'd also found in science fair competitions. I learned through these experiences that the fit of a school and its students is more important than the name, so I was very careful when I was selecting universities I wanted to attend. I listened to people's advice and then went with my heart.

2. What inspired you to create the early detection test for pancreatic cancer?

When I was still in middle school, a close family friend, who was like an uncle to me, passed away from pancreatic cancer. I was so sad and confused. I didn't even know what a pancreas was! I turned to every teenager's go-to resources when they don't understand something—Google and Wikipedia. What I found just shocked me. One reason the pancreatic cancer survival statistics were so grim is there isn't a reliable, inexpensive, and quick test to detect it when it's in the earliest stages and when the chances of being cured are better.

Armed with teenage energy and optimism, I decided to figure out a better way. I spent many months reading and printing out articles and thinking of ways to detect this cancer. I was in a biology class, listening to a lecture about antibodies and reading an article about single-walled carbon nanotubes, when I had a startling idea: what if I combined what I was reading about (nanotubes) with what I was supposed to be listening to (antibodies) and created a sensor to detect the antibodies to a protein that is thought to be overproduced in people who have pancreatic cancer! Of course, I had to read lots more and design an experiment to study the idea.

My parents were not supportive at first, because they liked the projects they could see, like the bioluminescent bacteria I used to study water pollution or the retrofits I created to improve dam safety. They thought I should change my project, but after seeing how much I was determined to study this, they started listening and encouraging me. Unlike my previous experiments, I couldn't study this idea at home—I needed real lab equipment and more expensive chemicals, so I decided to find a lab. I thought I could just send out my idea and sit back and wait for offers to work in labs to pour in.

3. You were turned down by 199 labs. What made you keep trying?

I was so naïve! I now realize how very busy researchers are and how long and tedious my initial emails asking for help really were. I didn't get too discouraged by the rejections I faced every day when I would return from school and check my email for answers. I'm embarrassed to say I didn't even have a professional-sounding email address, but one using a name of a favorite cartoon from elementary school. I learned from each rejection, improving my subject line for interest, making my email short and listing my limited credentials, and tweaking my experimental design. I wasn't sure if it would work or not. I remembered the statistics for pancreatic cancer and how many people died every day around the world from the disease, and I wanted to make a difference, however small, in those grim statistics.

4. What advice would you give teens who are trying to find their passion?
Try everything you can, and don't worry if you aren't good at first. I tried so many musical instruments, from piano, flute, saxophone, and clarinet to violin and cello. I was horrible, and no matter how much I practiced, I didn't improve much. I tried musical theatre and loved the friends and rehearsals but quickly found out I was not a good singer or dancer, and although I could make the cut in local events, it was clear to me that my talents would be better spent elsewhere. I tried many sports like baseball, lacrosse, and soccer, but I was more comfortable mountain biking or kayaking and using that time to relax and clear my mind.

I made the math team, and at first I thought I'd found my true passion—I loved the people and spent hours when I was supposed to be sleeping studying the Mathcounts and the art of problem-solving math books under the covers. The highlight of my summer was attending the month-long math camp I paid for by winning math competitions. I was obsessed . . . until I discovered science fairs and using the scientific method to examine and explain how the world works, and using that knowledge to find solutions to improve public health. I'm still thinking every day about ideas to make the world healthier and writing them in a journal to remember and refer back to.

My advice is to find your own path and think about what is important to you and makes you happy, and then work to improve your skills. Someone said to me, "What would you do if you woke up and it was Saturday morning and you had nothing scheduled for that day?" When you find the answer to that question, you are well on your way to finding your passion.

5. What's the greatest thing you've learned about yourself during this process?

I learned I am persistent and resilient, and those can be good qualities when combined with listening to good advice and following my heart and passion. I love to be around people who are trying to change the world for the better, improving the lives of billions of people, and who are impatient to get started working!

THE PRESSURE TO CONFORM

Have you ever done something just to fit in? Have you made changes to how you dress, act, or think in order to be like your friends? If so, you have conformed. This is not all bad. Some conformity is good, like following the rules at school, studying hard for tests, or showing up on time for all of your soccer practices. This type of conformity keeps things in order and establishes rules.

On the other hand, your true self may start to compete with the part of you that wants to be like everyone else. While you're trying to create your own identity, you may feel pressure to conform to what other kids are doing or how they dress. This goes along with a desire to fit in, blend, and not stand out. The value of blending in with the herd may seem worth it while you're in school, but as you get older, originality and creativity will be your greatest assets. As Alexandra Robbins stated in her book *The Geeks Shall Inherit the Earth*:

> There is too much pressure . . . to conform to a narrowing in-crowd image, when we should be nurturing the outsiders who reject that image. In large part, those are the individuals who will turn out to be the kinds of interesting, admired, and inspiring adults who earn respect and attention for their impact on their community or the world.[1]

Trying to be like everybody else. *I'm just going to go along with whatever my friends are doing.*

Remember Robbins's words while you're reading this book. Oftentimes the price of admission to certain cliques at school isn't worth the trade-off of changing the best parts of yourself. Appreciate your uniqueness and participate in activities that surround you with people who support you just the way you are. The closer you move to self-acceptance, the better off you'll be when it comes to handling peer pressure, bullying, and self-doubt. You'll feel awesome in your own skin and ahead of the game when it comes to pursuing your passions in life!

Spotlight
Ben Scheer, Photographer

Inspiration can be found anywhere. For Ben Scheer, his inspiration was found at home with his brother who has special needs. Frustrated with year after year of bad school pictures where his brother wasn't looking at the camera or smiling, high school senior Ben decided to use his love of photography to take pictures of his brother. His mom was thrilled when she received the pictures capturing the true essence of her son.

With the success of his brother's pictures, Ben decided to help other people who have a difficult time getting good pictures of their children. He created Photobilities to provide a place where kids with special needs can come to get their picture taken. They receive all the time and attention they need to capture their beautiful personalities. His work has been published by *The Whitman Journal of Psychology*, *Eidolon* magazine, and *Bethesda Magazine*. To view his photographs, visit photobilitiesphotography.com. By igniting his spark, Ben has helped many families enjoy pictures of their children!

WHO ARE YOU?

Who are you? It's a simple question but often a difficult one to answer. Or maybe you know the answer but are afraid to show people the true you. Knowing who you are isn't about knowing what kind of job you want to have when you grow up. It's not about your values or beliefs. It's more than what you look like or how you dress. It's not just one of those things—it's all of them!

You can look in the mirror and identify if you are short or tall, have brown hair or blond hair, or if you are curvy or thin. You were born with these features. You add your own personal sparkle to your appearance based on what you wear, how you style your hair, and whether you exercise or not. These are your physical attributes.

Your personality attributes refer to how you are on the inside. What school subjects do you enjoy? Who are your friends? Do you like sports? What are your beliefs? Are you shy or outgoing? Honest and kind? All of these things—and many, many more—define you as a person.

You, and only you, can choose the type of person you want to be, and you can do it right now. Don't waste twenty years (like I did). Don't waste even a second.

Think of yourself as a blank slate. Every time you try something new, you have the potential to light a spark. You can light thousands of sparks to become exactly the person you want to be!

Light your spark. *I'm going to keep trying new activities.*

Ignite Your Life Activity

We can be pretty hard on ourselves when it comes to our appearance, talents, and personality characteristics. Grab a pen and paper, and make a list to describe yourself on the inside and out. Next, make a list of how you would like friends and family to describe you in those same categories. Do the two lists match up? Are you realistic about how you describe yourself? Or are you a major self-critic? After you've read this book and completed the other activities, come back to this list to see if your opinion of yourself has changed. Hopefully, you will see that you're an amazing person!

2

IGNITE YOUR IMAGE

What matters is discovering myself under the veneer, under the
layers that are wrapped around me. There are two "yous"; there's
"you," the real you, and there's the image.

—Ted Dekker, Bestselling Author

ANYWHERE HIGH SCHOOL

Jack's alarm clock goes off at five thirty every weekday morning. After
pushing the snooze button a couple of times, he is always up by six.
Sometimes he squeezes off some push-ups and sit-ups before jumping
into the shower. After getting dressed and eating breakfast, he's out the
door by seven to pick up a couple of friends on his way to school.

Jack's sister Haley sets her alarm for five every morning and gets
out of bed immediately. Her first stop is to always look in the mirror to
see if she has any new blemishes. While she waits for the shower to heat
up, she steps on the scale and weighs herself. The number that appears
on the scale dictates the rest of her morning. If she thinks the number
is high, she has a hard time finding anything she wants to wear and she
hates her hair and makeup. She purposely skips breakfast but still ends
up late to school. If the number on the scale is low, then her morning

routine goes off without a hitch. She's happy with the way she looks, eats a good breakfast, and arrives at school on time.

HOW'S YOUR SELF-IMAGE?

You may think of your appearance when you think of the word *image*, but it includes a lot more than just how you look. It's the mental picture you have of yourself. It's how you think you look—if you think you're smart, talented, or a jerk. It's your perception, so it's not necessarily true. You may think you are ugly, horrible at sports, and boring, while others see you as cute, a great artist, and funny. If you have a positive self-image, then you see your assets first and your liabilities second. With a negative self-image, you focus on your imperfections and dwell on your failures.

Don't sell yourself short! The way you think about yourself will determine how others see you. In high school, I thought I was chunky, unremarkable, and average at everything when the truth was, I was funny, creative, and a really loyal friend. The way I felt about myself dictated how I looked to other people. Without self-confidence, I came across as awkward and shy. The only people who got to see the real me were a few really close friends.

A pretty face or six-pack abs will only take you so far if you're a jerk to people. On the other hand, if you have frizzy hair that's out of control, constant scrapes on your face from lacrosse, and a killer personality, you'll be more liked and attractive to everyone who knows you. You'll beat out someone who is superficial any day of the week when it comes to true

Appreciate the way you look. *I love my blue eyes, dark hair, and dimples when I smile.*

Always looking for flaws. *My stomach is so bloated, and don't even get me started on how huge my nose looks.*

friends. Eventually a person's personality and how they treat others will catch up to them. You have to match an inner beauty to your outer shell to maintain attractiveness to others.

Spark Quiz
How Do You See Yourself?

You may think you have a realistic view of yourself when in reality you're super hard on yourself. Sometimes it's difficult to know the difference. This quiz will help you to determine if your self-image is full of confidence or is clouded by insecurities. Answer *a* or *b* for the following statements to see where you fall on the Image Scale.

1. Monday morning you wake up with three new pimples. You
    a. Think they make you even more awkward looking.
    b. Put skin cream on them and decide it's a good day to wear a hat.
2. Your friends call and ask you to meet them at the pool. You
    a. Decide the last thing you want to do is be near your friends in a bathing suit.
    b. Think it sounds like a lot of fun and don't think about how you compare in a suit.
3. Your best friend makes the school soccer team. You
    a   Fixate on how it doesn't seem fair because you stink at all sports.
    b. Get excited to congratulate your BFF.

4. You get a 90 percent on a book report when you're used to getting 100 percent. You
   a. Feel like a complete failure.
   b. Figure out where you lost points and then forget about it.
5. In school you'd rather
   a. Be like everyone else and blend in.
   b. Be yourself and not worry about everyone else.

If you answered mostly *a*, then it's time to work on improving your self-image. Start appreciating everything that makes you great. Everyone is born with their own unique set of looks, talents, intelligence, and gifts. It's hard to find those things if you're focused on your flaws. Stop comparing yourself to other people and enjoy being you. Make a list of the things you like about yourself, and take the time to love yourself.

If you answered mostly *b*, then you've got a healthy self-image and understand the benefits of being yourself. This can change during different times in your life, so continue to appreciate your good parts and don't go looking for bad stuff.

Illuminator: Caitlin Boyle, Operation Beautiful

In 2009 Caitlin Boyle was fed up with the negative self-talk people do regarding how they physically look. With scraps of paper and a pencil, she launched a movement by writing *You Are Beautiful* and posting the notes on restroom walls, mirrors, and at the gym. Now thousands of people have joined her mission by posting notes in random places all over the world. Her motivational speeches tackle body image issues like photoshopping, self-esteem, and how to a have a healthy lifestyle. She is the author of *Operation Beautiful: One Note at a Time*, and *Healthy Tipping Point*. To find out how you can contribute to a positive body image, visit operationbeautiful.com. Read on to learn how Caitlin is changing the way people feel about themselves one Post-it Note at a time.

1. What is Operation Beautiful?

The mission of Operation Beautiful is to post positive messages in public places for strangers to find. Since the site's beginning in June 2009, I have received over twenty thousand notes from all over the world.

2. What experiences did you have as a teen that influenced you to create Operation Beautiful?

I grew up in Miami, Florida, where there is a heavy emphasis on appearance and money. For a long time, my perception of what was valuable was highly distorted by this atmosphere. I spent a lot of years thinking that you had to be perfect to be worthwhile.

3. How are body images distorted in the media?

I think it's important for teens to understand that the way men and women are presented in the media—the muscular ideal and the thin ideal—are created so "normal" people feel bad about themselves and feel compelled to buy a product or watch a TV show. The purpose of distorting body images in the media is really to drive consumerism. If you feel good about yourself the way you are, you won't buy those things.

4. How does this affect the way people think of themselves?

We're holding ourselves to an impossible and unrealistic standard, which hurts your self-esteem and—in turn—damages the rest of your life.

5. How can teens have a healthy body image?
Focus on finding a healthy balance and remember that health looks different on different people. There are a lot of different shapes and sizes, and all are attractive and worthwhile. Being self-confident in who you are and what you can do is the most appealing (and important) thing of all.

6. What's the difference between a healthy lifestyle and one that is consumed with exercise and dieting?
It's all about attitude. When I trained for a Half Ironman (a triathlon involving a 1.2-mile swim, a 56-mile bike ride, and 13.1-mile run), my life was totally consumed by exercise and eating, but it was a short-term goal that I was trying to reach. An unhealthy obsession might be one that you cannot break away from. Also, if your thoughts stop being logical (such as, *I'm tired, but I have to continue running until I reach five miles because two isn't good enough*), you may have a problem.

7. What activities can a teen participate in if they aren't naturally athletic?
Everyone can find a physical activity that suits their tastes. Maybe you love to dance—try Zumba. Maybe you like quiet alone time—try yoga. Maybe you love to be outside—try going for long walks.

8. If you could go back and give advice to your teenage self, what would you say?
Stop being so hard on yourself, and look for more opportunities to help others. Helping others is so important.

A TALE OF TWO JUSTINS

You may feel like people either have it or they don't when it comes to good looks, popularity, talent, and intelligence. You may think you have very little control over how people will perceive you, but that's not true. Let me tell you a little story about two guys named Justin and you be the judge.

Justin Timberlake was discovered at the age of eleven when he sang on the talent show *Star Search* and then became a member of *The Mickey Mouse Club*. From ages fourteen to twenty-one, he was part of the popular boy band called *NSYNC that sold over 50 million albums. Since then, he's launched an even more successful solo career and has expanded into acting, winning nine Grammys, four Emmys, seven American Music Awards, and eleven MTV Awards.

Justin Bieber has a similar story. He was discovered at age twelve when his mother posted a YouTube video of him in a local singing competition. At age thirteen he sang for Usher and landed a recording contract. He plays piano, drums, guitar, and the trumpet and has played to sold-out shows all over the world. By age twenty-one, he'd already won one Grammy, eight American Music Awards, twenty-three MTV Awards, and sixteen Teen Choice Awards.

They sound pretty similar, right? They are both good-looking, talented young men who have spent a lot of time occupying the teen heartthrob space. This is where their similarities end. While the news of Justin Timberlake's personal life has centered around his marriage, appearances on talk shows, and what designer labels he's wearing, Justin Bieber's personal life has been a lot more colorful. In order to distance himself from his teen idol image, he began hanging out with people who had a reputation for getting into trouble. The headlines spent more time focused on his misbehavior than on his music. He was arrested for vandalism, reckless driving, driving under the influence, and assault. His bad-boy behavior did not garner him respect but instead gave him the label as "2014's most annoying celebrity."[1] These two Justins both started their careers with the same talents and image, but under their own control, they went in two different directions.

BODY IMAGE

Do you ever stare at your reflection in the mirror and start critiquing the way you look? You might think, *I am so fat, I look too scrawny*, or *My skin is so oily*. If you do this, you're not alone. Most people notice their flaws first and their good parts second. As a teen, your body is constantly growing and changing, which makes it even harder to have a realistic image of yourself. One day you might have pimples, and the next day your skin is flawless. Add to it body hair, voice cracking, and body odor, and puberty starts to sound like a real drag! Don't worry—everyone goes through it. When it's over, you'll look less like a kid and more like a young man or woman.

Understand it's unfair to compare yourself to pictures in the media. *I like seeing pictures of my favorite celebrities, but I don't measure myself by them.*

In the meantime, lighten up on yourself and treat yourself like you treat your friends. You wouldn't tell your best pal they are fat, ugly, or weird looking. If you did, you wouldn't have a friend for very long. Treat yourself with the same respect by turning your negative self-talk into positive statements. "I hate that I don't look this way" can become "I love that I have my own look and am different than everyone else." The things you don't like about yourself now will be the things you love about yourself later.

THE MEDIA MYTH

You've seen the pictures—the ones that taunt you from magazine covers and websites with flawless skin and amazing bodies. They are celebrities, athletes, and models both male and female. They create an impossible standard for you to live up to, because the people you are seeing in the pictures aren't from the real world. They have personal trainers, nutritionists, dermatologists, and plastic surgeons. Before the photographer takes a single picture of them, they meet with a makeup artist, hairstylist, and fashion stylist. After the pictures are taken, the real work begins. Software programs like Photoshop allow designers to make improvements or changes to the pictures. They can change skin coloring to hide pale skin or pimples. A skillfull graphic designer can replace a bald head with a full head of hair, erase wrinkles, and whiten teeth. Lately, media and advertisers have been criticized for using software to create six-pack abs, shave off pounds, and

Comparing the way you look to how your favorite celebrities and athletes look. *I would give anything to look like my favorite TV stars.*

make women look more feminine and men more rugged. Sometimes the trend is for women to be curvy, and at other times rail thin. Men may be shown as big and bulky, or as tall and slender. Either way, the industry ideal is constantly changing. The result is an illusion that is meant to sell you products and magazines, not promote self-esteem.

Illuminator: River Ceballos, Actor, Model, and Spokesperson

River is a professional actor, model, and spokesperson on teen issues. He has been called the male Demi Lovato for his work in activism regarding body image issues and youth insecurities. He works with the Jed Foundation, Love Is Louder, Proud2BMe, National Eating Disorders Association, Men Get Eating Disorders Too, and My Life My Power. He was a celebrity panelist at the screening for the documentary *The Mask You Live In* about how masculinity is defined for boys. His work in the modeling industry and as an actor gives him a unique perspective on how body image is shaped by the media and why those expectations are unrealistic. After battling an eating disorder, he learned how to truly appreciate his body. Read on to learn how River is redefining beauty in the modeling industry.

1. Tell me about your teen years.

In my early teens, I was extremely heavy and awkward. I was very much comfortable being in the shadows. I was really into the arts—acting, writing, photography—I was never a jock or looked at as masculine. After my parents divorced, I definitely went through that teen-angst phase where I acted out, rebelled, and didn't really fit in with one specific group. I was a misfit. A lot of things were out of my control at this point, especially my home life and family situation. The only thing I felt I had control over was my weight.

2. How are male and female body image issues different?

I don't think they are that different, to be completely honest. I think female body image issues are more well-known; they're okay to talk about. There are so many female celebrities that have opened up about their body image struggles, and we know about so many female support groups and such . . . but men don't really have that. Men feel like they have to always be the alpha male. They have to be muscular, in shape, macho, buff, but there aren't too many sources we can turn to or places where we can open up about this without being deemed a pussy or gay. Eating disorders are still viewed as a female disease.

3. What would you say to teens who feel their bodies don't measure up to their peers?

I'd say to love yourself. I've ruined my body and will forever live with ailments because of the damage I've caused to my organs over the years. This is all because I wanted a body that looked like the jocks did. I went to extreme lengths to achieve this. I used to envy every boy who could walk around the locker room with his shirt off and not get laughed at. Instead of being the best version of myself and achieving the best body for me. I wanted a football player's abs, a soccer player's legs, and a bodybuilder's arms. Truly being comfortable in your own skin is the most beautiful feeling. There's nothing like it. Your body is *yours*, so love it, cherish it, treat it right, and it will reward you.

4. How can people learn to accept their own uniqueness?

Surround yourself with people who love you for you. Being different is beautiful. All the things and personal features I was embarrassed about when I was younger are what I get the most compliments on now. I love my style, my look, and that's because it's purely mine. You aren't meant to be a replica—you're an original, a limited edition. Remember that!

5. If you could go back to give advice to your teen self, what would it be?

I'd tell my teen self it will all work out, it'll be okay, and I'm a lot stronger and smarter than I give myself credit for. I'd say to love yourself. The bumps in the road ahead are just stepping-stones. Don't sweat the small stuff; you're a kid. You aren't supposed to have everything figured out. Enjoy life; enjoy your youth.

6. How does the media affect how we feel about how we look?

I'm in an industry where it's okay to dissect people. It's almost like they have a free pass to critique you. With Photoshop and glam squads being the norm, it's incredibly easy to feel ugly compared to people we see in the media. I have one foot in that world, so I see the smoke and mirrors, the hair and makeup teams, and the lighting effects. When I do a photo shoot, people will stop me and say, "OMG! You look great. I wish I looked like that!" And I reply, "I wish I looked like that too." Ha-ha, it's not real. Perfection isn't attainable. Humans are not meant to be perfect. Don't try living up to those expectations.

GO FOR SOMETHING LARGER THAN YOUR LOOKS

Do you base your self-worth on how you think you look? If so, then you're building your self-confidence on a faulty foundation. All it takes is any doubt about your appearance to cause all of your confidence to come crumbling down, whereas if you tie your self-confidence to what you appreciate about yourself and your inner beauty, then you're working with a solid foundation. Any doubts you have about your appearance will seem minor compared to the happiness you have with your daily life.

When you connect to things outside of yourself, it puts things into perspective and makes it easier to focus on your internal self more than your external packaging. You are so much more than the appearance of your body parts or the numbers on the scale. Pursuing a meaningful life that focuses on your dreams and life enjoyment will help you to push any body image issues aside. Here are a few practices to get you in the right mind-set for a meaningful life.

✳ **Choose happiness.** Have you ever heard of the saying "Fake it till you make it"? Sometimes it's hard to find anything to smile about, and at other times it's hard to stop grinning. Your inner self and outer self usually share similar feelings. If you're having a great day because you got an A on your test, got asked to a dance, and are done with your homework, then chances are, other people will notice a smile on your face and a little pep in your step. If your day has been a disaster, then think of some reason to smile—whether it's a joke you heard last week, a gift you're getting for your best friend, or a cuddle with your pet. The act of smiling will automatically make you feel better.

✳ **Toughen up your body.** To get positive energy flowing, practice breathing techniques and body-strengthening moves through yoga. Yoga is relaxing and helps with flexibility, strength, and balance. You will practice very distinct poses that require you to quiet your mind of negative thoughts and focus on your body movement. Any time you are nervous or upset, try the calming effects of yoga to help get your emotions under control.

✳ **Find your inner peace.** Meditation is a great way to clear your mind and get rid of the stress from the day. Find a quiet place to sit or lie down and close your eyes. Focus on inhaling and exhaling through your nose. Empty your brain of thoughts, and think only about your breathing. Start by doing this for a few minutes a day and work up to thirty minutes as your concentration gets better. There are many different ways to meditate, so do a little research online to see what works for you.

WHAT DOES SPIRITUALITY HAVE TO DO WITH ANY OF THIS?

When it comes to spirituality, many people think it has to be tied to a specific religion. They automatically connect it to a church, temple, or synagogue. For some of you this may be true, and for others it may be a different kind of journey. So what does it mean to be spiritual? It means you are on an inner path to self-discovery about your beliefs and how you choose to live. You may have heard of searching for the meaning of life or connecting to something bigger than ourselves. You form this connection with yourself, other people, animals and nature, or a higher power.

Judging people by how they look. *I would never put my picture on Instagram if I looked like that.*

Practicing spirituality reminds you that life is made up of so much more than your body parts. When you focus on how you look, you can fail to see the beauty that exists everywhere. It's easy to spend time noticing what your body doesn't have—whether it's six-pack abs, a flawless complexion, toned legs, or something else. When you focus on living a spiritual life, your world gets bigger because you realize life has a lot more meaning than how you look. When you feel terrible about your appearance, you have a narrow view of the world because you stop paying attention to everything else around you. Spirituality can give you a sense of purpose on how to connect with the world. Here are some questions to ask yourself when considering the big picture and spirituality.

✳ What three qualities do I value most in people (for example, love, kindness, and respect)? Does appearance make the list?
✳ Do I love and respect the people in my life any more or less based on how they look?
✳ Who do I admire most and why?
✳ Do my thoughts focus on the world around me or just on myself?
✳ Am I a good person?
✳ What gives my life meaning?

Ask yourself some of these questions the next time you look in the mirror. Be on the lookout for your inner beauty. When you treat yourself with compassion and love, you can begin looking at yourself with an appreciation for what makes you unique. Your world will expand when you use a spiritual eye to view what's truly important in your life.

Spotlight
Chantelle Brown-Young, Model

You wouldn't expect a contestant on *America's Next Top Model* to have spent her childhood being bullied for her looks. Or have memories of being called "zebra" and "cow." The name-calling began when the skin condition vitiligo caused Chantelle Brown-Young to develop white patches on her face and body. But this didn't stop her from pursuing her dream of becoming a model and walking the runway. Her inner and outer beauty has kept her in hot demand. She's traveled the world on modeling assignments and has been featured in fashion magazines. By embracing her uniqueness, she has become a role model. To learn more about Chantelle, also known as Winnie Harlow, visit her website at chantellewinnie.com. By igniting her spark, Chantelle inspires young girls to appreciate their differences!

IT'S ALL ABOUT A FULL LIFE

Your body is only a small part of who you are. Put your time to good use and try to live life to the fullest. Find activities you love to do where time stands still. Hang out with people who make you laugh and see your inner beauty. You'll forget all about how you look when you're doing something fun.

You are unique. From your head to your toes, everything about you is 100 percent different from anyone else. Embrace all of those differences. They provide the packaging for your inner beauty to shine through. When you feel good about yourself, it shows on the outside. Give yourself the chance to radiate from the inside out.

Compliment your friends. *Chris, I think it's cool that you get up every morning and run three miles before school.*

Ignite Your Life Activity

It's time to work on your image. If you were a celebrity right now, what suggestions would the president of your fan club have for you? Would they tell you to stop making negative comments about your weight? Or obsessing about how ugly you think you are? Or finding flaws with your talents? Take all the negative things you say about yourself and turn them into positive statements. For example, *I'm so short* can be turned into a positive statement by thinking of the advantages you have by being small, like *I can use my size to dodge my opponents during a soccer game,* or *I can always find clothes I like.* Or, *I'm too tall* can have advantages like *I always stand out in a crowd* or *It gives me an advantage for playing basketball.* Act like you are your own personal fan club president and you are recruiting new members. Now that you've got a recipe to increase your star power, take your self-image to the next level. It's your time to shine!

3

IGNITE YOUR FRIENDSHIPS

I realized that bullying never has to do with you.
It's the bully who's insecure.

—Shay Mitchell, Actress

ANYWHERE HIGH SCHOOL

Every day Marcus, Rish, Jacob, Diane, and Amy eat lunch together. On Tuesday, Marcus is noticeably absent from their table.

"Where's Marcus?" asks Amy. "I saw him in algebra this morning, but I haven't seen him since."

Jacob motions for the group of friends to lean in, so he doesn't broadcast his news to the entire table. "You guys didn't hear about him and Tina?"

"Where have you guys been? I've been getting texts about it all morning," Diane says. "She totally dumped him!"

Rish and Amy look surprised. They hadn't heard the news. "Poor Marcus," Amy says.

"What a chump!" says Jacob. "She was always out of his league. I bet she was using him for something—maybe help with her homework."

"I never could figure out why she was dating him," Diane says. "Maybe she actually met a guy that's good-looking."

"Man. You guys are jerks. Instead of feeling bad for him, you're totally trash-talking him," Rish says as he gets up to leave.

"Wait up, Rish. I'll go with you," Amy says. "I want to find Marcus and see if he's okay. Breaking up is bad enough, and having everyone talk about it makes it even worse."

YOUR FRIENDSHIPS HELP SHAPE YOU

Did you know that your friendships help to form your identity? Who you are as a person is shaped by those around you. When you meet new people, you might be introduced to someone who is of a different gender, race, sexual orientation, nationality, or religious belief. If you take the time to get to know these people, your beliefs or ideas about your identity may change. You can learn so much from your friends.

You naturally pick up traits and behaviors from the people you choose to spend time with. This can be good and bad. One of my best friends in high school was a vegetarian and environmentalist. She taught me to be less wasteful and more aware of my effect on the planet. It's not something we ever really talked about, but I picked it up by just being around her.

Not seeking out the right kind of friends. *I'll hang out with the first group of people that accepts me.*

Everywhere you go, you have the opportunity to meet new people. Your parents and family members are only one piece of the puzzle of creating your own identity. Part of understanding who you are is figuring out where you fit in with people your own age. Be open to expanding your group of friends. You never know—the next person you meet could have a huge impact on your life and take it in an entirely new direction!

Tips for Being a Good Friend

✳ **Be you.** There's nothing worse than feeling like you have to act or dress a certain way to fit in. Stay true to yourself and be you. If that's not good enough for your friends, then maybe you're not hanging out with the right people. Find the friends who like you for you, and don't want to change you. Being fake shouldn't be your only option!

✳ **Stick up for your friends.** If someone starts gossiping about one of your friends or teases them in front of a group of people, what do you do? Do you stand back silently and watch? This is your moment to be a really good friend. It's not easy to speak up, but you'd want someone to do the same for you. Have your friend's back. Someday they may be watching yours.

✳ **Don't feed the machine.** Rumors and gossip gain momentum every time someone repeats them. Don't divulge your friends' secrets or add fuel to the fire by participating in gossip. The internet extends the reach of rumors and can make them last longer if people keep spreading them. Extinguish the flame by staying away from all gossip. Whether it's your best friend, your nemesis, or a perfect stranger, no one deserves to be the object of negative chatter.

✳ **Look out for your friends.** Your friends may make some really poor decisions, and there are things you can do to help them out. Here are some examples: Never let your friends get in a car with someone who's been drinking. Keep to the buddy system when you're out together. Help keep them out of harm's way. Your friends might not always want to hear what you have to say, but sometimes they need to hear it anyway. You'd want someone to do the same for you!

✳ **Lend an ear.** Sometimes listening to a person is the best way to show you care. Whether your friend is stressed about their grades, worried about a family member, or having relationship problems, they will appreciate having a caring friend listen to their concerns. Who knows? Someday that same friend may be doing it for you.

Spark Quiz
What Kind of Friend Are You?

Before you start examining your relationships with other people, you must first assess your own personality. How do you rate as a friend? Are you a giver and not a taker? Would you be described as caring and accepting? Do you pay attention to what your friends tell you, or do you smile and nod as you think about other things? Take this short quiz to see what kind of friend you are and where you might need to make improvements.

1. How much do you know about your closest friend's family?
   a. Are you kidding me? I know everything.
   b. We don't really talk about our families.
   c. I kind of zone out when they talk about their family.
2. Do you and your close friends have a lot in common?
   a. We share the same values and are loyal to each other.
   b. We're close because we like the same activities.
   c. I can't think of anything we have in common.
3. If a friend calls you about a problem, what do you do?
   a. I listen, discuss it, and check in on them later to make sure they're okay.
   b. I let them talk it out before moving on to another subject.
   c. I listen while texting another friend at the same time.
4. How often do you compliment your friends?
   a. I say nice things to my friends all the time.
   b. I notice great things about them but forget to mention them.

    c. Not much.

5. If a friend asked to borrow five dollars, what would you do?

    a. Give it to them.

    b. Lend it and find out when I'll be paid back.

    c. Tell them to get lost and get a job.

6. What would you do if one of your closest friends started avoiding you?

    a. I'd hunt them down and find out what's wrong.

    b. I'd give it a little time before I approached them.

    c. I'd leave them alone and hang out with someone else.

7. What do you do if you think your friend's significant other is a bore?

    a. I'd keep my opinion to myself—at least they're happy!

    b. I'd avoid doing things together as a group.

    c. I'd tell them.

8. What would you do if you heard your friend was talking behind your back?

    a. I wouldn't believe it. It's just a rumor.

    b. I'd have a chat with them.

    c. I'd move on. They're obviously not the right friend for me.

9. How do you celebrate a close friend's birthday?

    a. I get a group of friends together and plan a great evening.

    b. We have a mini-celebration the next time we get together.

    c. I post a "happy birthday" message online.

10. If your best friend joined the school soccer team, what would you do?
    a. I'd go to the games when I'm available.
    b. I'd congratulate them.
    c. I'd be bummed I'd have to hang out with someone else.

If you answered mostly *a*, then you're good to your close friends and most likely have some pretty cool and supportive pals in your life. It's better to have a few really good and trustworthy relationships than a whole slew of people you can't count on. Make sure your friends value you and offer you the same level of attention you give them.

If you answered mostly *b*, then you might be juggling a lot of friends. You can strengthen relationships by being available when your friends need someone to listen. Don't be afraid to invest time and effort in the people who are important to you.

If you answered mostly *c*, then you are more guarded in your relationships. Maybe you've been burned before or you don't like showing or sharing your feelings. If this works for you, it's not a problem, but you may need to open up when you start dating. If your relationships are unsatisfactory, try increasing your level of effort.

Illuminator: Jason Li, Founder, iReTron

Have you ever moved or transferred to a new school? Jason Li has. He knows what it's like to join school activities and build a network of friends around them. Those activities taught him new skills and how to work with different types of people. His sophomore year of high school, he broke his back and started reading about social entrepreneurship to fill his time while recuperating. He came up with the idea to help people recycle their old electronics by selling them to his company where he finds a way to reuse them. This allows them to have a positive impact on the environment and earn some extra cash.

The idea took off, and some big people took notice! During his senior year of high school, Jason appeared on the show *Shark Tank*, spoke at TEDxTeen, and was named the Next Teen Tycoon by Vertical Response. From there, he went on to become a student at the University of Chicago and major in economics. His newest corporate venture is called UProspie, which allows high school students to connect with college students to learn about the schools they're interested in attending. To find out how you can recycle your old electronics, visit iretron.com. And if you're looking for college advice, head over to uprospie.com to meet up with students attending your favorite colleges. Read on to learn how this high school student started his first socially responsible business.

1. What activities were you involved with in high school?

I came into a new high school not knowing anyone. In an effort to make friends, I joined the largest club on campus, which happened to be speech and debate. As a freshman, the captain mentored me through writing speeches and acted as an amazing role model. By the time I was a junior, I was cocaptain with seniors and organized our team's first-ever out-of-state tournament. Speech and debate taught me so much about public speaking and leadership.

Because I was a new student, I wasn't able to receive a spot in Saratoga High School's Intro to Journalism class. I had a passion for photography that I'd developed in middle school, so I decided to email the journalism teacher. After becoming a freelance photographer for the school's yearbook, I joined as part of the staff and was able to skip the intro class. Perhaps it was the inner entrepreneur within me, but I wanted a way to display my art while contributing to something bigger.

By junior year, I was quite active in student government. At Saratoga, we had these Quad Days, when each grade decorated a section of the school and put on a play for one lunch period. It was more or less a competition, but it was simply a good spirit tradition for the week of homecoming. Just like any other class, my grade included some hooligans who were young and just liked to have fun. Because I was new to the school, I wasn't very popular, so I never got involved in student government. After two consecutive years of major mistakes that disqualified our grade for homecoming competitions, I decided I wasn't going to be a bystander anymore. As a student of the class of 2014, I wanted to represent [as a student officer] myself and my peers well.

2. How did these activities help you to connect with other people?

These activities were amazing because as an underclassman, I was unafraid of reaching out to the upperclassmen for help or guidance. I kept telling myself, "You're just a freshman. You're supposed to be dumb, so don't be afraid to ask dumb questions." I simply had nothing to lose. Because I was a young student, people were very willing to help me. As I grew to be an upperclassmen, I remained humble and hungry for new knowledge, but at the same time, I enjoyed helping others reach their goals, whether it was in speech or in yearbook.

3. How did you come up with the idea for iReTron?

iReTron was really the amalgamation of many ideas, the first of which was a personal goal of mine. I was interested in business, but after trying many clubs on campus, I realized they were mock style and had a lot of hand-holding. I wanted to try something real, so I had the aspiration to create my own company.

My world geography teacher taught us about the e-waste crisis. Living in Silicon Valley, I was surrounded by technology and couldn't help thinking about how all of this would one day contribute to the e-waste crisis. I felt a need to change things and find a green solution. During this time, I was part of a volunteer group where we would go out and plant trees or do gardening work. To be honest, I did it for the volunteer hours. I realized this and asked myself if this made me a bad person. It was then that I realized that going green isn't easy. Driving is easier than biking. Most people would rather watch TV than wake up on a Saturday morning and plant trees. It's financially difficult to install solar panels on houses and buildings. After identifying these problems, I wanted to find a rewarding and easy way for people to go green. What if people could get paid for reusing their electronics? What if people who needed to upgrade products could hand their older versions to people who can't afford the newest models? I felt I was on to something!

Around the same time, I learned about social entrepreneurship, which is when people utilize business models to do good for the environment or society. I remember on Sunday nights in middle school, I would ask my parents for thirty dollars for lunch money for the week. At first it was fine, but soon it didn't feel right to keep taking my parents' money since I knew how hard they worked to earn it. I wanted a way to be sustainable by myself. After that, it came together and I started my business of buying, fixing, and selling phones. With $2,000 of initial funding from my father, I was able to book a speaking gig at the Green Festival, America's largest environmental festival, and have some initial capital for the business. It got bigger as time went on, and we built a website after winning multiple competitions—winning a total of $43,000. iReTron then launched nationwide and gained national recognition by some major publications. After two and a half years of hard work, I was approached by a producer from ABC about being a contestant on the show *Shark Tank*.

4. What challenges have you faced while setting up a company?

The biggest challenge was trying to compete and partner with adults while I was a kid. Although there was a ton of support from people, it took a lot for adults to pay me any real attention. I thought I had to start acting more adultlike and speak like them. After nearly three years of conditioning myself to take up my adult persona when representing iReTron, I had trouble being myself when talking to businessmen. My *Shark Tank* producer always pushed me to be a kid, but I was very skeptical because I was afraid of not being taken seriously as a thirteen-year-old kid.

5. What advice would you give teens who are trying to find their passion?
I think it's incredibly hard to find your passion, so don't be too hard on yourself if you don't know yet. I realized the best way to find your passion is to not look for it directly. Instead, identify problems that you care about. If you care about them enough, try to find a solution! Not everyone gets excited about photography or the e-waste crisis as much as I do. With problems at every corner of our lives, we need to see them as opportunities. They don't have to be big problems either. Maybe your passion lies in meeting new people. In a way, that's what Brandon Stanton does with Humans of New York. Maybe your passion lies in helping people travel and you could do something like Airbnb. After you find that interest, your niche, go all out to pursue it. Maybe it won't work, but too often young adults give up for other people. Never give up because someone else tells you to. Only when we free ourselves from external pressures do we pursue what we truly love. And if, internally, you lose interest in something, then move on and find out what's next for you!

6. What impact has pursuing a dream had on your self-confidence?
My dreams are big, but I am small and I embrace that. I know I can't singlehandedly fix the e-waste crisis, but I am confident enough to try. When you pursue a dream, you can't help but be addicted to it. You almost forget about everything else. I sometimes work on iReTron instead of going to parties. I sometimes pull all-nighters and forget about the time. Sometimes I go a full day without eating just because working on it brings me so much pleasure. I don't need to be recognized

for it. Publications and TV are nice, but what makes me really happy is doing something I really enjoy.

NEGATIVE NELLIES, LIP FLAPPERS, FAKES, AND GOSSIPS

Everyone knows someone who's the drain of the party—the person who knows how to rain on everyone's parade with negative words or grumpy moods. With just a few words or facial expressions, they suck the oxygen right out of the room. Sometimes these people are our friends. Other times they're people we are forced to put up with because they're family members, classmates, or coworkers. Knowing how to identify these types of people and how to deal with them will help you avoid being sucked into their toxicity.

The Negative Nelly

Otherwise known as Debbie Downer, Bobby Bummer, and Grumpy Gus, this person spends a lot of time complaining. If you say you're going to take a bike ride, they'll tell you it's going to rain. Going to a movie? It's probably sold out. They have an eagle eye for problems but don't offer any solutions. They're the constant victim. When they don't make the basketball team or a club, or don't get hired for a job, it's because the coach/president/manager had something against them from the beginning. This is because they're never responsible for their own failures or mistakes; it's always the conditions that caused the problem, according to them. When dealing with a Negative Nelly, you have two options: ignore their negativity or ask them how they would solve the problem.

The Lip Flapper

Otherwise known as the One-Upper, the Topper, and the Attention Hog. This person can hear a story you tell and respond with a similar experience—but always with a larger outcome. If you went on a family vacation to the beach, then they went to a nicer beach with parasailing,

Jet Skiing, and surfing. Did you get an A on your algebra test? They got an A, too, but also completed a science project, attended swim team practice, and saved a family of five from a house fire the night before the big test. Bottom line: you can't win. Contrary to what you may think, they aren't competing with you. This is all about their insecurities. When confronted with a Lip Flapper, it's best to ignore the boasting and change the subject. If it's a close friend and it really bothers you, then have a one-on-one conversation with them. They might not even realize they are doing it.

Fakes and Gossips

Otherwise known as Phonies, Motormouths, and Imposters. These are the people who talk behind your back, share your secrets, and act like your friends but often don't really like you. When you're sharing your biggest secrets, they're wondering who they should tell the news to first. When you're the most devastated or upset about something, they don't want to hang out with you—unless they're wringing you out for every juicy detail. These people elevate themselves socially by stepping all over everyone else. Once again, self-confidence and self-identity come into play here. These people don't know who they are and how to feel good about themselves, so they climb on top of other people by pushing them down. Don't waste your time with people who are disloyal. If it's a family member or someone you often see, then watch what you say. You never know who they could repeat it to.

Being a phony, backstabber, or user. *If someone better comes along to hang out with, then I'll ditch the person I'm with.*

ARE YOU IN A TOXIC FRIENDSHIP?

Does your friend make passive-aggressive comments like "I can't hang out with you on Saturday because some of us have to earn what we spend"? Or are you the butt of embarrassing jokes when other people are around? Do your plans together get ditched if something better comes up? If so, you may be dealing with a toxic friend.

How to Deal with Toxic Friendships

Having a toxic friendship can be exhausting and hurtful. It's also infectious. It's difficult to keep a positive attitude when you're surrounded by negativity. It's easy to ignore a negative person if you aren't friends, but what do you do if your friend is the person who is toxic? Do you tell them, ditch them, or ignore the issue?

With so many varying degrees of behavior, there's no correct answer to these questions. You have to evaluate your friends and find out why they do what they do. If they're bad-mouthing you, revealing your secrets, or putting you through emotional or physical harm, then it's time to ditch

> Seek out loyal friends. *I'd rather have a couple of awesome friends in my life than a ton of fakes.*

them. If their toxicity veers more toward self-criticism, bragging, and complaining, then you'll have to make a decision. You can discuss the issue with them, ignore it, or spend more time with other people. Relationships are supposed to be a reciprocal arrangement, so if your needs for true friendship aren't being met, then there's nothing wrong with hanging out with someone else.

What If You're the Toxic Friend?

What if you're the person who does some of these things? Most people at some time in their lives have been complainers, have hurt someone's feelings, or have repeated gossip. How do you turn it around if you've fallen into this trap? The easiest way is to put yourself in your friend's shoes before you act or speak. How do you want to be treated? If you want your friends to be positive, happy when you succeed, and trustworthy, then you need to treat them the same way. Mimic the behaviors you appreciate in other people, and eventually they will become second nature.

Illuminator: Lee Hirsch, Writer and Director, The Bully Project

In 2011 filmmaker Lee Hirsch released his award-winning documentary, *Bully*. This film captures the lives of five families who are affected by bullying, following their lives over the course of one year starting with the first day of school. Hirsch, who was bullied himself as a kid, started a nationwide movement of awareness called The Bully Project on behalf of the 13 million youth bullied every year. This campaign works to end bullying by creating awareness and training materials for young people, parents, and educators. To see how you can be involved, visit the campaign's website at thebullyproject.com. Read on to learn how it took only one person with an amazing idea to spark a movement.

1. What can kids do to bully-proof themselves?
Keep looking until you find someone who will have your back, because eventually you will. If your parents don't have your back, if your teachers don't have your back, if your principal doesn't have your back—you will find someone if you can keep asking for help from someone who will stand with you and help you rebuild that confidence.

One of the things you can do is to let go of whatever you think social success is. You might have to align yourself with other kids who are on the outs and build those friendships. A lot of kids, when they're bullied, want to be at the top, and they don't recognize there's a place for them [in the middle], where they can start to build their confidence with other kids who are outsiders. They will probably treat you way better and you'll have a real friendship, as opposed to trying so hard for acceptance from the kids who might be the jocks or the popular group.

Be strategic. Be yourself. You're a survivor. Now be strategic about getting help and getting friends.

2. What would you tell a kid who is afraid to tell an adult about bullying because they don't want to get anyone in trouble?
When you can't cope, you need to tell somebody. When you feel unsafe, you need to tell somebody. If it's the first time something's happened, then maybe you don't need to tell somebody. Here's a bullying list: bullying is an imbalance of power, it's repetitive, and there's bad intent. If those three things are happening, then you need to tell somebody, and if they tell you it's a not a problem, don't accept it.

3. What precautions can a person take in how they use their cell phones, computers, and so on to avoid cyberbullies?
Don't fan it, and don't play into it. If it doesn't have oxygen, it's not going to spiral out of control. Cyberbullying gets really bad when it's spiraling and other people are feeding into it and it's piling on. If you see it, jump on it and report it. There are good reporting tools now.

4. What steps can people take to empower themselves after being bullied?
Try to find things where you can excel. Join a music group, be in a chess club, or do theater. Work to find those places where you feel safe and thrive. Find ways to connect. Find a community.

HOW DOES BULLYING WORK?

Bullying comes in many forms. It can be physical with pushing, shoving, and tripping or verbal, where words are used hurtfully with name-calling, teasing, or spreading rumors. Online bullying happens when bullies use texting and social media to attack their victim. Bullying involves the bully, witnesses, and the victim.

The Bully

Where do bullies come from? Why do they act the way they do? Some bullies were once victims themselves, so they take their hurt and anger and direct it toward their peers. Or they model the behavior of someone else, like a parent or sibling. People think it's more desirable to seem cool or strong than face possible rejection. This could contribute to why they're so insensitive to other people's feelings.

Bullies take the easy way out when it comes to getting attention and making themselves feel more powerful. Instead of doing this through positive ways like building achievements, being kind to others, and working hard, they use fear and intimidation to get people to notice them. This may be to elevate their status or popularity or to take the focus off their own imperfections. Most bullies don't give a lot of thought as to how their actions and words affect their victims. Some bullies who become aware of how hurtful they are do change how they treat others, while others will continue to bully into adulthood.

Bullying other people. *I think it's funny to intimidate underclassmen.*

The Witness

An active witness has the biggest opportunity to end bullying. Witnesses collectively have a lot of influence over the severity and acceptance of bullying. Without an audience, bullies don't get the attention they're typically seeking. An active witness is someone who stands up to a bully by speaking up and letting the bully know they are not okay with the situation. They can make a real difference because sometimes it only takes one person to put an end to someone getting bullied.

A passive witness is someone who doesn't stand up to a bully because they're afraid of becoming a target themselves. Many times they feel helpless and uneasy around bullying but don't know what to do.

Because people are standing around quietly, a bully may think bystanders agree with the way they're acting—or think it's funny. If you aren't comfortable confronting a bully, then there are still ways you can help. You can find a teacher, talk to a guidance counselor, or gather support from other peers. Act the way you would want someone to act for you.

Help other people. *I won't stand around and just let someone get picked on.*

The Victim

A person who is being bullied might have rumors spread about them, receive threats, be physically abused, and be humiliated online. Sometimes bullies choose people who are passive, physically weaker, and don't have a lot of people to stick up for them. Other times they choose their target out of jealousy. They may envy your grades, your relationship status, your talents, or your family life. Basically, a bully is looking for any type of reason to put a person down.

So what are your options if you're being bullied? Just like a bully requires an audience to encourage their bad behavior, you need similar backup. Find a parent, teacher, or trusted friend to talk to about what's happening. Join an organization or club where you meet new people who share your interests. Build a tribe of support. If you can't find those people in your community, then find them online. Dig into the resources in the back of this book and get some help. So many people are on your side. Being bullied is never your fault! What may seem impossible right now will get better!

Spotlight
Breanna Mendoza, Survivor of Bullying

The bullying of eighth-grade student Breanna Mendoza grew so severe, it became life threatening. She was born with a rare condition called Goldenhar syndrome, which left her with a facial defect impacting her hearing, vision, and respiratory system. One punch to the face could block her airways and prevent her from breathing, so she left school before the bullying could get physical.

She decided to share her story with her local news station and the story went viral. Immediately messages of encouragement and love started pouring in for Breanna. The story made it all the way to the Children's Craniofacial Association in California where she and her family were invited to a complimentary retreat where she could meet other teens with her condition. One local businessman heard her story and started the Breanna Project to provide her with a special day that included clothes, a trip to the salon, guitar lessons, and a limo ride to a Taylor Swift concert. Another family in her community volunteered to pay her tuition to attend a private school, where she was welcomed with open arms. By igniting her spark, Breanna stood up to the bullies at her school and inspired others to do the same.

WHO IS YOUR TRIBE?

Your friendships with other people say a lot about your self-identity. If you are self-confident, you are more apt to spend time with supportive, loyal, and trustworthy people. You seek out relationships with people who share your same interests and values. You may have a shared history, or you could become brand-new friends.

Your identity is linked to the company you keep. Other people will try to categorize you by the people you associate with, so choose people who are worthy of your friendship.

When new people come into your life, put them through a mental checklist. Will this person be a good friend? Do they have the same values as me? Will they lift me up instead of putting me down? Can I rely on them?

You can make the decision who to trust with your friendship. Invest your time with people who appreciate the real you. Be yourself. You will find your people!

Ignite Your Life Activity

Think of all the qualities you value in your friendships. Are loyalty, honesty, and supportiveness on the list? Do you gravitate to people who share your interests, like athletics, clubs, academics, or other activities? Maybe you look for someone who makes you laugh and is easygoing. Write down your ideal friendship want list. Now think about the kids you know from school and your neighborhood. Is there someone who has these qualities and is struggling for a friend? Try reaching out. Who knows? You might find your new best friend.

Surround yourself with positive people. *I don't hang out with people who are always negative.*

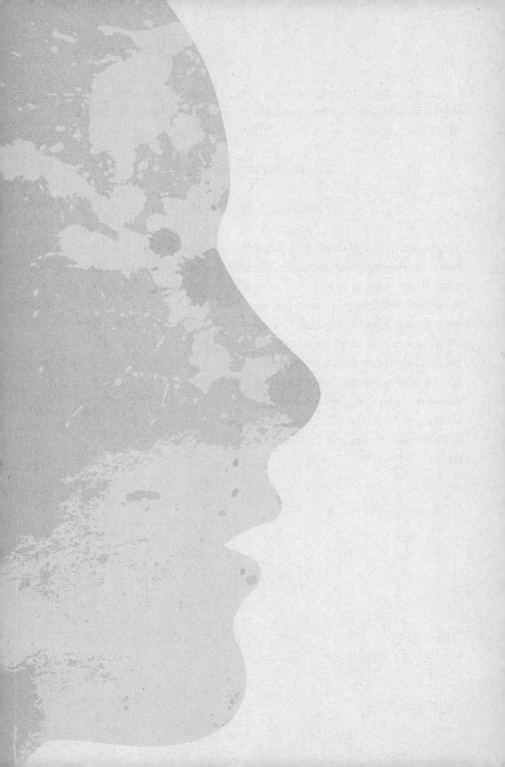

4

IGNITE YOUR RELATIONSHIPS

*A relationship can give you a gut-wrenching feeling sometimes.
It's a real emotional ride.*

—Drake, Performer

ANYWHERE HIGH SCHOOL

Friday at school everyone is talking about how Jeanna told Charlie she will never date him. It's bad enough when she says no after he asks her out, but it gets even worse when she tells all her friends. By Saturday it is being discussed on Instagram. Later at dinner, his parents notice how quiet he's been all weekend.

With his best friend out of town, Charlie decides to talk to his dad. "Hey, Dad, can we talk about something?" he asks. "I've got a problem with a girl and her friends."

"What's going on?" His dad joins him on the couch.

"I asked this girl out a couple of days ago, and she kind of laughed and said no. What's even worse is that she told everyone about it," Charlie says.

His dad looks like he wants to say something but decides to listen instead. He can tell there's more to the story.

"Now it's all over the internet. They're making me look like a total loser." Charlie hands his phone over to show his dad some of the postings.

His dad's gut reaction is to get mad, but he knows that won't help the situation for his son. So far none of the posts mention his son by name but tease Jeanna about a boy who asked her out. "It looks like three different people are making these posts. Are these people you're friends with?"

"No, they're Jeanna's friends. I don't even know them."

"What about Jeanna? How do you feel about everything with her?" his dad asks.

"I really liked her. We've always talked in class, so I don't know why she's acting this way."

"As far as her friends go, I wouldn't give them the time of day. They haven't mentioned your name, and if you jumped into the conversation online, you'd just start something," his dad says. "Jeanna is a different story. She's your friend, so if you're comfortable with it, I'd give her a call and see what's going on with all of this. Don't do it by text but through a conversation. Maybe she'll tell her friends to back off if you talk to her. Do you think you could call her?"

"I can try. We've talked on the phone before about school and stuff," Charlie says. "I don't think she'll be a jerk if her friends aren't around."

IT'S NOT THE QUANTITY BUT THE QUALITY OF YOUR RELATIONSHIPS

Relationships play a key role in helping you define who you are. A strong family can provide the foundation for your support system, and a significant other can give you encouragement and appreciation, while strong mentors like coaches, teachers, and employers can teach and inspire you to pursue your dreams. These important people in your life should be supportive, honest, attentive, and trustworthy. They are there for the good times and especially when things get tough. When you are happy, sad, or lonely, they are the first people you want to call. It's a misconceived notion that you need a ton of people in your inner circle. It's not the quantity but the quality of the relationships that makes the real difference when igniting your spark!

Encourage the people in your life. *I think it's great my sister is trying out for volleyball.*

TYPES OF RELATIONSHIPS

In addition to friendships, it's important to include other types of relationships in your life. You gain something new from every person you let into your life. Whether it's unconditional love, advice, or true romance, relationships help you to grow.

Your Family

Your family includes people you are related to by blood, a marriage, or adoption. You probably spend most of your time with them and share the strongest bond. Families come in all shapes and sizes and should be supportive, loving, and respectful.

Shutting your parents out of your life. *I wish my parents would just leave me alone.*

Your Mentors, Teachers, and Coaches

Other relationships are with people you look to for education, advice, and training. You might encounter them at school, work, or during an activity. They provide experience and guidance and become a valuable resource as you are growing as a person.

Your Partners

Partners, or significant others, are people that you have an emotional and physical connection to. They are a part of your life by choice and attraction. A healthy romantic relationship allows you to be yourself and will make you feel respected.

Spark Quiz
Is Your Relationship Healthy?

The key to a healthy relationship is mutual respect. You can demonstrate this by being supportive and taking an active interest in each other's lives. Some other characteristics of a healthy relationship are trust, honesty, and patience. This is true whether the relationship is with a family member, friend, mentor, or romantic partner. Answer the following questions with *true* or *false* about the person in one of your current relationships.

1. They encourage me to pursue my interests.
   True or False
2. They make me feel good about myself.
   True or False
3. They listen to me when I have a problem.
   True or False
4. They are liked by the other people in my life.
   True or False
5. They are supportive of my other relationships.
   True or False

6. They text or call to check in on me.
   True or False
7. They share their life with me.
   True or False
8. They are kind to other people.
   True or False
9. They give me room to do my own thing.
   True or False
10. They are someone I like to hang out with.
    True or False

If you answered *true* to most of the questions, then you are in a healthy relationship. You respect each other and have room to grow as individuals. Remember that relationships are a two-way street, so show your partners, friends, and family members the same level of support they offer you.

If you answered *false* to many of the questions, then it's time to look at the warning signs of a potential problem. Examine your answers and see if you can recognize any unhealthy patterns. Sometimes it's just a matter of communicating and telling someone what you want. Encourage them to do the same. If the relationship is right for you, then an honest discussion will only make it stronger.

Illuminator: Denny Locascio, Owner, Impact Fitness

Denny Locascio helps young adults build character both inside and outside of the gym. As the cofounder of Impact Fitness, he helps athletes train their bodies and minds for competition. Some of his clients can be found playing in the NFL, in MLB, and as college and high school

All-Americans. He uses the education he received in exercise science from the University of South Florida and the inspiration from past coaches in his job as a strength and conditioning coach. You'll find only positivity in his gym, where ten-year-olds can be found doing push-ups next to professional athletes, and where character is measured by hard work and grit.

1. Why did you choose to work with young athletes?

I chose to work with young adults for many reasons: I feel they have the biggest opportunity to be influenced, my personality tends to connect well with a younger generation, and I feel the best way to positively influence future generations is to start with the younger generation that will influence the future.

2. How has a good coach or mentor impacted your life?

The two biggest mentors in my life were both my grandfathers. They taught me so much about work ethic, toughness, grit, love, family, and respect. After my grandfathers, I would say a mix of coaches have been the next greatest mentors in my life—from my high school wrestling coaches, football coach, college strength coach, and other coaches in the fitness industry. Again, the common lessons all these men taught me were about work ethic, toughness, and a love for learning. One of the greatest lessons I learned was from Mark Asanovich, who told me, "People don't care how much you know until they know how much you care."

3. How has hard work both on and off the field helped you grow as a person?

I put so much value into teaching and instilling hard work into kids because hard work has been one of the biggest building blocks in my life. There is a TED Talk with Rick Warren, where he asks what we're doing with what we've been given. I believe I owe it to myself, God, family, and friends to work as hard as possible with the gifts God has given me. I would not be where I am today if I did not embrace hard work and put forth the effort needed.

4. Do you think teens should focus on being themselves or worry about fitting in?
We should always focus on being our best self. One of the quickest ways to depression is getting caught comparing yourself to anyone else. The only person you can compare yourself to is yourself from the past. You have to learn to run your own race.

5. If you could go back and give some advice to your teen self, what would it be?
I would write down all the stories from my older family members. Once they pass, you will lose those stories forever unless they have been journaled. I am not a person that likes to change the past, because it is what made me who I am today. I embrace the life lessons, learning opportunities, and challenges of my youth, and I'm thankful for those times.

KEYS TO A HAPPY RELATIONSHIP

* **Bring something to the table.** We all know people who are takers and are only interested in what will help them. Practice giving people what you want to receive. If you want someone who is trustworthy, then don't gossip or break people's confidence. Model the behavior you like in others.
* **Know your self-worth.** When you value yourself, then you can be an equal partner in your relationships. You are deserving of love and respect. Your wants, needs, and personal beliefs matter, so don't be afraid to express yourself.

Listen to the people who are trying to help you. *I'm going to take my teacher's advice and look into taking a coding class over the summer.*

✳ **Talk it out.** The key word here is *talk*. Yelling never helps any situation. Take some time to think about what you want to say before you open your mouth. It's easy to say things in the heat of the moment that you later regret. Relationships have ups and downs, so learn to handle conflict calmly.

✳ **Learn how to apologize.** If you are wrong, own it! Everyone makes mistakes. To properly apologize, say, "I'm sorry," and take responsibility for messing up. This shows that you respect the other person's feelings and want to set things right.

✳ **Beware of the green-eyed monster.** Jealousy is terrible for relationships. The key to fighting this monster is trust. If you're constantly spying on each other's texts and social media accounts, or if you're worried about what's going on when you're not around, then you need to have an honest chat.

✳ **Ask questions and listen to the answers.** Relationships grow as you get to know each other. Having someone take interest in your hopes and dreams is amazing. Conversations with people let you share the best of times and can help you through your hardest moments.

✳ **Have fun.** Cheer each other on, celebrate the small things, and share lots of laughs. Find things you love to do together, and make the time to do them. Nothing can improve your relationship—and health!—faster than spending time having fun.

SIGNS OF AN UNHEALTHY RELATIONSHIP

Let's face facts: it's hard to see the flaws in your romantic relationship when you're in the thick of it. It's fun to be part of a couple—to be around a person who likes you—when you can't wait to see each other every day.

But let's get real: not all relationships are created equal. Some are super supportive, where you become better people by just being together. Others might hold you back and keep you from being yourself. Your family and friends may have an opinion about your relationships too. It's hard to be objective when your emotions are involved.

Problems in a relationship can be small things that are a little annoying, like texting too much or arguing over movies. Or they can be major issues, like not wanting you to spend time with your friends or acting overly jealous. Here's a list of potential red flags that could be too serious for you to ignore.

Build your relationships on trust. *On Friday nights my partner and I each hang out with our own friends.*

* **You feel like you need to change the core of who you are to make another person happy.** It's great to be in a relationship where you try new things and have new experiences. You might start watching a new series on Netflix, or become a fan of racing go-karts. It becomes a problem, though, if you start thinking, dressing, and acting like your partner because they want you to change.

* **According to your partner, you can't do anything right.** In any relationship, but especially in a romantic relationship, look for people who build you up. Someone who constantly puts you down, is overly critical, and calls you names is not treating you with the respect you deserve. These statements will eventually chip away at your self-confidence and make it difficult for you to believe in yourself.

Quitting activities you enjoy. *I'm going to stop playing in my band because my partner thinks it's stupid.*

* **Your partner is holding you back.** You may be a go-getter who likes to get good grades, be involved in school activities, and lead

an active social life. Your partner might have a relaxed attitude about school and prefer to just hang out in their free time. If your relationship is keeping you from reaching your goals, then you may need to decide if this is the person for you.

* **You don't trust them or vice versa.** Trust is a huge part of any relationship. No one wants to be looking over their shoulder to see if someone is gossiping, flirting, or talking bad about them behind their back. If you find yourself spying on texts and questioning your partner's every move, then trust is an issue. Is it your insecurity causing the problem, or is your partner giving you a reason to be suspicious?

* **Your partner wants to be with only you.** You feel like you spend all your free time together, and they don't think they see you enough. Meanwhile, your family and friends complain you're never around. If you feel like your partner is putting the squeeze on you in person, on the phone, or through constant texting, then it's time for a talk. In any relationship, every person needs room to breathe and time to be alone, with friends, and with family.

* **You don't share the same values.** Your values and beliefs are the foundation of who you are. From an early age, you start developing your beliefs on what is right and wrong. They are your guiding principles for how you act. Maybe you value honesty, equal rights for everyone, and family loyalty. If your partner is less than truthful, prejudiced, and doesn't treat their family with respect, then you may have a hard time seeing eye to eye.

* **Your relationship goes from adoration to obligation.** Relationships are supposed to be fun and exciting. A few disagreements are normal, but when it becomes mostly drama, then it's time to take a step back to see if it's worth fixing. Chances are, your partner is thinking the same thing. Have a talk and see if it's time to make up or break up.

WHAT TO DO IF YOU ARE IN A BAD RELATIONSHIP

There are varying degrees of bad that can occur in any type of relationship. Some of these things you can fix, and some might require outside help. You may have a difficult time communicating with your parents, a teacher who is uninspiring, or a partner who is never happy. These are things you may be able to fix. You can try talking to your parents to tell them your point of view. You can seek out a mentor or coach to inspire you at school. And if your partner is never happy, then maybe it's time to let them go. Then there are the really *bad* types of relationships, where someone is treating you in a harmful way. These can be with a family member, a coach, or a partner. You may be scared of this person or feel like you need to act a certain way so they don't get angry. It's important to understand the signs of abuse and how you can get help.

What Is Abuse?

Abuse is when someone hurts you on purpose. Whether you're a guy, a girl, young, or old, it can happen to anyone. Their goal is to have power over you and to control how you act. This happens through physical, emotional, or sexual abuse. The important thing for you to remember is that it's never your fault! Learn how to identify abuse and how you can get yourself out of a bad situation.

There are three main types of abuse:

* Physical abuse is any type of violence, like hitting, kicking, smacking, and pushing.
* Emotional abuse is the use of bullying, teasing, humiliation, and issuing threats to make you feel bad about yourself.
* Sexual abuse occurs when someone is forced to do anything physical they don't want to do.

What should you do if you recognize this behavior in one of your relationships? Trust your gut; it won't lie to you. You may feel like you don't deserve any better or that you caused the abuse. That's not true! Abusers want their victims to feel guilty, ashamed, and scared. They are counting on you to remain silent. Find an adult you trust, like a parent, guidance counselor, or health professional, to confide in. It's important for you to have help breaking away from your abuser. Your safety is the most important first step. To get outside help and support, contact an abuse crisis center or teen help line. For a few options, look at the resource section in the back of this book.

Illuminator: Eileen Kennedy-Moore, PhD, Psychologist, Author

Eileen Kennedy-Moore is an expert on friendships and parenting. In addition to being a counselor, she is also the author of several books such as *What About Me? 12 Ways to Get Your Parents' Attention*, *Raising Emotionally and Socially Healthy Kids*, *Smart Parenting for Smart Kids*, and *Growing Friendships*. She has appeared as an expert on the *Today* show and other television programs. For advice on teen issues, visit her website at eileenkennedymoore.com. Read on to find out how this psychologist works with parents and youth.

1. How do relationships help form our identity?

The important people in our lives can help us feel known and accepted. They are like mirrors that help us gain perspective on who we are and who we want to become. People who know our flaws and love us anyway help us see ourselves with kinder eyes. People who believe in us help us find the courage to grow.

We also create our identity by choosing to spend time with certain people. When we hang out with one group and not another, it's like we're declaring, "I'm like them! This is where I belong!"

Relationships help us move past ourselves. When we comfort a friend or cheer for a teammate or help a classmate, we're stepping beyond self-interest to become part of a broader community.

2. What are some of the biggest challenges young people face in discovering who they are?

Three challenges I often see are:

* Being too good at knowing what others want or expect. When people are very good at figuring out what others—teachers, parents, peers—think they ought to do, they sometimes have trouble hearing their own inner voice. Knowing what others want is useful and important information, but creating our own identity means figuring out what matters to us.

* Focusing on what they're against rather than what they're for. It's easy to be critical or rejecting of others. A harsh, judging stance can make people feel superior, but it's a shallow answer to the question, Who am I? Rather than criticizing others, it's harder but more meaningful to discover and take steps toward what we value.

* Letting fear hold them back. Fear of looking foolish can stop teens from trying new things or even saying what they think. Anxiety isn't a stop signal. It's a sign you're doing something new or challenging, which is the only way to grow.

3. How can teens form happier relationships with their peers?

Choose kind friends. It's easy to get caught up in popularity and status, but pay attention to how you feel when you're with your friends. Good friends leave you feeling happy, supported, and accepted.

Assume good intentions. If your friend does something you don't like, try to imagine some reasons for this behavior other than deliberate meanness. Maybe it was an accident. Maybe your friend just didn't realize how it would affect you.

4. What advice would you give teens who spend a lot of time arguing with their parents?

Often, the best way to get people to change how they treat you is to change how you treat them. Try to see your parents as people rather than obstacles. How are they feeling? What do they care about? How can you respect that?

Build up the positive side of your relationship: Tell your parents one thing about your day. It doesn't have to be a big thing. Maybe your friend told a funny story, or your math teacher wore a ridiculous tie, or your favorite performer has a new song. Simple sharing can help build connection.

5. If you could go back and give advice to your teen self, what would it be?

Tolerate uncertainty. It's okay not to know. Trust yourself and keep going. The answers will come.

Spotlight
Shaun Verma, Founder, MDJunior

Have you ever done any volunteer work? Donated food? Participated in a fun run at school? Or dropped off some toys for Toys for Tots? Have you ever walked away wishing you could do more? This happened to Shaun Verma at age ten when he was helping the Red Cross after wildfires had left thousands of people homeless and hurt. The long lines for medical attention stuck with him. He wanted to do more, so he created the organization MDJunior with the mission of "inspiring selfless service through mentorship" by creating "future leaders in the field of medicine and healthcare through the youth of today."[1]

Shaun pairs up middle and high school students with medical professionals for mentorship. Many of these student chapters are located in schools with high dropout rates. The students are encouraged to finish high school and pursue higher education in healthcare fields. At monthly chapter meetings, members meet visiting mentors, attend teaching seminars, and visit hospitals. A large part of MDJunior is to also teach students the importance of giving back to their community by volunteering at health-related nonprofit organizations. By igniting his spark, Shaun has decreased student dropout rates, introduced new students to the medical field, and helped communities with volunteer assistance! To see how you can become involved, visit his website at mdjunior.org.

LOVE THE ONES YOU'RE WITH

Who are the important people in your life? Do they cheer you on or put you down? Do they support you and make you feel good? Knowing your value and self-worth can help you choose wisely when it comes to investing your time with someone. Nobody wants to be in a relationship that drags them down.

Treat people the way you want them to treat you. It sounds too simple to be true, but it works. Give your mom a hug in the morning, bring soup to someone who is sick, and remember the birthdays of the people you love. These are all examples of ways you can strengthen your relationships.

Strive for a good mix of relationships with people who can help support and encourage you. Your family members, friends, mentors, and even romantic partners can inspire you to reach for your dreams. Think of them as your personal trampoline—if you fall, they will lift you up, and when you need a little bounce, they will provide the springboard. All you need to do is jump!

Dating anyone who asks. *I don't care if we don't get along; it's better than being alone.*

Ignite Your Life Activity

Every relationship you have has an impact on who you are and whether you feel encouraged to pursue your interests. One of your most important relationships is with your family but often FOMO—fear of missing out with your friends—can keep you from spending quality time with the people you live with. It's important to nurture these relationships because your family is the foundation of who you are. They are the people who will stand with you during the good times and will hold you up during life's challenges. Schedule some individual time with family members who support you. They might be your parents, siblings, grandparents, or anyone you consider to be family. It can be as simple as eating breakfast or taking a walk together in the evenings. They will be thrilled when you take the initiative to spend some quality time together to talk and strengthen your relationship.

5

PUT THE SPARK iN SCHOOL

What's amazing is, if young people understood how doing well in school makes the rest of their life so much [more] interesting, they would be more motivated. It's so far away in time that they can't appreciate what it means for their whole life.
—Bill Gates, CEO of Microsoft

ANYWHERE HIGH SCHOOL

"Hey guys, how was school?" Gislaine and John's mom calls out from the kitchen as they walk into the house.

"Great, Mom," Gislaine says, hurrying to her room. She has a hundred people to text and email about an upcoming pep rally she is planning. On top of that, she has a ton of homework to do for her honors classes. Gislaine is always busy but doesn't mind it because she loves school.

Meanwhile, her brother, John, grabs a snack and heads to the basement to play video games. He's done crappy on another biology test and doesn't feel like getting a lecture from his mom. His grades are proof he shouldn't waste his time studying. He knows he can't measure up to his sister. Why should he care about school anyway? *They just teach a bunch of stuff I'll never use in life.*

HOW DO YOU FEEL ABOUT SCHOOL?

By now you've been going to school for many years and may still have some years ahead of you. You might be a true academic who loves school for the sake of learning. You might be a student who can't wait for the weekends and counts down the days to summer vacation. Once you get to a certain age, it takes more than just showing up and being smart to get good grades. Homework, projects, and tests take up a lot of time, and your teachers' expectations are high. This is why some people love school and others can't wait for it to be over. Whether you dread your alarm clock going off in the morning or bound out of bed feeling refreshed, let's look into how you can make the most out of your school day.

Make school meaningful.
What can I get out of school this year?

Spark Quiz
How Serious Are You about School?

Whether you love school or aren't a huge fan of it, school is here to stay. School is the first step toward your future. Every semester brings you closer to graduation, college, or a career. Take this short quiz to see if you're taking full advantage of the opportunities school offers you to learn new things.

1. In general, I like going to school.
   True or False

2. I figure out a way to use my school projects as a way to learn more about my interests.
    True or False
3. I complete my homework and study for tests.
    True or False
4. My classes are challenging enough and not too easy.
    True or False
5. I have one or more teachers I would consider as mentors.
    True or False
6. I'm involved in school activities either through clubs, academics, or athletics.
    True or False
7. School is helping me work toward my goal of college, a job, or starting a business.
    True or False
8. Academic achievement is important to me, not just to my parents.
    True or False
9. I read books and go online to read about things that interest me.
    True or False
10. School is important to my friends.
    True or False

If your answers are mostly *true*, then school is very important to you. You realize school is a stepping-stone for bigger and better things. Classwork and grades are something you work hard at, and you realize the value in giving your best effort. Expose yourself to as many new learning opportunities as possible during this time. Who knows? You may stumble upon a new passion or a future career opportunity.

If most of your answers were *false*, then it's time to figure out a way to make school work for you. Try to make your school years productive. A positive academic experience can get you one step closer to doing what you want to do. Sometimes the social scene of school can be distracting. Keep in mind that in a few years, you and your classmates will all scatter in different directions. Your future will always be with you, so take some time to set yourself up for future success.

Illuminator: Noa Mintz, Founder, Nannies by Noa

When it came to spending time with the perfect babysitter, Noa Mintz wasn't happy with her options. She wanted someone who spent less time on their phone and more time doing activities with her. At the age of twelve, she decided to solve her problem by launching Nannies by Noa to help people find the perfect sitter. She became her own teacher by researching online how to start a successful business. Her hard work paid off when her agency became the go-to place for matching caregivers with families. National television shows and publications like the *Today* show, *Squawk Box*, *Teen Vogue*, and the *New York Post* have interviewed Noa about her success as a small business owner. To find more about her company, visit her at nanniesbynoa.com. Read on to learn how this teen places babysitters and nannies with families in New York City and the Hamptons.

1. Where did you get the idea for Nannies by Noa?
The idea for Nannies by Noa came from my own experiences as a New York kid. A real entrepreneur encounters a challenge and then

tries to solve it. That is exactly what I did. My mom had used many different platforms to try to find good babysitters, with no success. Agencies were sending her sitters who were not engaging and interactive. They were the kind of nannies that would sit on the bench at the playground and not go down the slide with the kids. I wanted to provide NYC parents with engaging, fun, and energetic nannies. That is at the core of Nannies by Noa.

2. How did you know how to start a business?

Truth be told, I will never know how I was able to do it. It is not so easy. I think it is all about intuition and motivation. My largest platform for learning how to run the business was learning from other businesses. Being an entrepreneur, you have to be creative in how you gain knowledge. I studied their websites and written materials, read about their mistakes and strengths, and used that as my way of learning and creating my own business school curriculum. As entrepreneurs, we are learning every day, and that's part of the beauty of what we do. Teaching yourself is not something you get to do in every career. It's just one of the many reasons I love being an entrepreneur.

3. What challenges have you experienced along the way?

I've had to deal with people doubting me because of my age and not believing I was capable of doing something like this. I was not always treated with respect by my peers. But by trying to bring me down, they actually brought me up. Because I have learning differences and don't always do well in school, my peers found it hard to believe I was capable of starting, much less succeeding at, a business. Also, throughout this journey, people have doubted me (clients, other agencies, babysitters), but I learned that success is all about patience, and trust comes eventually. It was extremely difficult to balance school and the business and hanging out with friends. I struggled with maintaining this balance for a while, but finally I learned how to be efficient and not procrastinate, which allows me to run the business, focus on school, and have fun with my friends.

4. *What have you learned about yourself during this process?*
So, so, so much. I have learned that I am an executer. I don't just dream. I do. I've learned that I need to be confident to be successful. If I am not confident, people will have hesitations about using Nannies by Noa and won't believe in me.

5. *What advice can you give teens who are trying to discover their passions?*
Explore different hobbies and passions even if they aren't considered cool by your peers. Try them out and give them time. Seek inspiration from the environment around you and the people you are surrounded by. If you have a dream, be willing to change it. Dreams will evolve over time as you have more life experiences and discover new interests.

6. *What's next for you?*
Gosh, I don't know! I will continue working hard at my business. I want to finish high school and go to college. I want to go into a career where I can utilize my creativity and motivation. I want to continue to be able to wake up every day and be excited for what lies ahead. Even though my dream is to grow Nannies by Noa to be the world's leading child-care agency, I am willing to change that dream as I learn more about myself and what makes me happy. Perhaps I will decide to do something else eventually. I am open to different things. I want to continue doing community service and having time for friends!

SPARK UP THOSE PROJECTS

By now, I bet you've noticed you have a project, essay, or upcoming test for at least one of your classes at all times. Most of this work is done after school hours and tends to eat into your free time. Maybe you'd rather hang out with friends or take part in activities you enjoy. This makes it difficult to be excited about doing schoolwork. The key to enjoying school is finding a way to apply what you're learning to your everyday life or toward something you would like to do in the future. This makes the learning process easier and a heck of a lot more fun.

Here's an example on how to do that: Your language arts teacher asks you to write a five-page biography on someone you admire. Since you play basketball, you decide to write your paper on an NBA player. Right now you are having a difficult time with your three-point shot, so you decide to write your paper on Stephen

Take advantage of school projects. *I'm going to write my history paper on Frank Lloyd Wright, because I think it would be cool to design houses one day.*

Curry, who is known as a great three-point shooter. During the research for your paper, you watch his videos, read interviews, and learn how he developed his game-winning shot. You start incorporating his drills into your own practice of basketball, and soon you notice your shots are beginning to improve. Your passion for the game shows in your writing, and the teacher gives you a great grade. By incorporating something you love to do into your homework assignment, you've managed to learn a new skill, get recognized for your effort, and enjoy the learning process so much more.

A CORNUCOPIA OF CLASSES

Have you noticed the older you get, the more options you have in your class selection and after-school activities? In elementary school you most likely had one main classroom and spent a couple of hours a week in music and physical education class. Middle school is a big transition where you start to change classes every hour and have the opportunity to be inspired by many different teachers. You are expected to be organized and to stay on top of your homework. You have to juggle many different teachers with different rules and expectations. Don't worry, it gets easier. Keep in mind that all of your classmates are in the same boat. After school you can bond with your classmates by joining a team sport or participating in a club.

Picking classes just because you heard they were easy. *I'm going to find out which classes have the least amount of homework.*

By the time high school rolls around, (hopefully) you are an old pro at working with different teachers and keeping on top of your homework assignments, because you've got much more exciting things to focus on. This is the perfect time to explore your interests and try new things. Most high schools let you pick your classes, so even within your main subjects of math, science, and language arts you are able to choose a specialty. You will have access to a whole list of elective courses like culinary arts, graphic design, photography, theater, and accounting. You don't have to be an athlete to find something to do after school. High schools have all kinds of clubs. Academic clubs like the Honor Society, debate team, and student government are popular. If you're looking for friends who share a common interest, then you may find them in clubs like anime, environmental conservation, Ping-Pong, or a book group. Can't find what you're looking for? Then start your own club! This is your time to take charge and identify your interests. Consider school your opportunity to try new things.

ONE SCHOOL—MANY, MANY PERSONALITIES!

Becoming aware of the many personalities in your school will help you to appreciate that every person is different. Whether it's at school, at a job, or in your neighborhood you will always be surrounded by new people. You may feel like you have nothing in common with some of these people, but it's important to get along with different people and embrace their uniqueness. Don't stereotype. Their appearances may be deceiving. That outstanding jock may be a book club member, or the disruptive kid could be a shy guy in one-on-one situations.

Appreciate the different personalities at your school. *I like getting to know people who are different than me.*

People are rarely two-dimensional and have a lot more going on than you see at school. If you appreciate them as individuals, then you'll feel more comfortable being yourself too. Read through the following list of typical school personalities. See if you can appreciate what makes them different:

* The new guy, often considered mysterious and interesting
* The disruptive kid who everyone loves
* The one who makes everything a competition
* The gossip
* The person with a social cause
* The one who gets all As without studying
* The person who appears to have everything
* The president of every activity
* The school spirit diehard
* The person with an amazing talent
* The jock
* The party thrower
* The floater who fits in with every school clique
* The teacher's pet, often smarter than the actual teacher
* The musician
* The gamer who loves computers
* The goth

* The introvert
* The comedian
* The heartthrob everyone is secretly in love with

Illuminator: Adora Svitak, Writer, Speaker, Advocate

In 2010, when Adora Svitak was twelve, she gave a TED Talk titled "What Adults Can Learn from Kids," which has now been viewed millions of times. Since then she has spoken at hundreds of conferences, in classrooms, and at the United Nations Economic and Social Council Youth Forum. She's written three books and is the organizer of the event TEDxRedmond. *Pacific Standard* magazine named her one of the 30 Top Thinkers under 30. In 2011 she received the National Education Association Foundation's award for Outstanding Service to Public Education. When most teens were learning to drive, she was starting her freshman year at UC Berkeley. To watch her videos or read her blog posts, visit adorasvitak.com. Read on to learn how Adora took control of her education and turned learning at school into a collaborative experience.

1. Why do you think you've accomplished so much at such a young age?
I don't ever look at myself and think, *Wow, I'm so accomplished*, so this kind of question is always a little hard for me to answer. But I think that gut reaction of, *Well, I'm not that accomplished*, is actually part of the answer; having the humility to never think that you've accomplished so much drives you to continue achieving, creating, and dreaming. Stay humble and you stay hungry for the next big thing.

2. How can students who are bored or dread sitting in class every day find inspiration?
I was that student for a large part of my own high school experience, and I think it reflects terribly on our education system that it's extremely

normalized for students to say, "I hate school." Personally, I tried to pursue a lot of independent projects within the confines of class. If a teacher didn't tell me about the applications of a new piece of learning, I would find them. Also, it can be hard, but you have to see your teachers as so much more than dispensers of information; try to see them as people to bounce your big ideas off of, and as learners alongside you. Some of my best conversations have been the ones I've had with teachers in the few minutes before or after class. It's possible to find inspiration even in the most uninspiring of circumstances if you see everyone around you as a resource.

3. What does it mean to you that students can be the recipient and author of their own education?
I'm a huge proponent of lifelong learning, and to my mind, a big part of that is being comfortable with teaching yourself and others. Too often students are painted as only the consumers in education—teachers dispense information, and we receive it—but I want to see a much more active model of learning, where we have the chance to provide input for major decisions, help with curriculum design, and lead independent learning projects.

4. I know you delivered a TED Talk in 2010 about this, but what are your feelings now about what kids can teach adults?
As I've grown older (and more jaded), I think the importance of knowing what kids can teach adults has become even clearer to me. I've confronted a lot of moments in my life where I've stared cynicism and accepting the status quo in the face and said, "No, I'm not going to take that—eleven-year-old Adora wouldn't." Among my friends and, I think, among high school and college students in general, there's this unfortunate association of cynicism with higher intelligence and sincerity/idealism with a certain foolishness deserving of pity (you know, the way everyone feels when they watch *Mr. Smith Goes to Washington*)—I want

to try to combat that. It's an odd combination, but the kid inside me keeps me from taking myself too seriously and encourages me to take other things more seriously—that is, I keep making poop jokes and standing up for what I believe in.

5. What do you do when you run into roadblocks?
I listen to angsty music on Spotify. Or rap. If you follow me and you see that "Adora just listened to 'No Church in the Wild,'" you'll know I'm really trying to kick a bad case of writer's block.

Questionable music preferences aside, in a broader sense, I think that I just kind of accept that a roadblock is there and try to not stress too much. One of my favorite mottos is "This, too, shall pass." When I was twelve and thirteen, I went through (as lots of kids do) some pretty bad emotional turmoil, and the worst part for me wasn't the acuteness of depression as much as the illusion of permanence, the feeling that it would never end. So, I remind myself that everything in life, the best moments and the worst, are ephemeral (short-lived), and I think of the name of this movie I once watched: *Someday This Pain Will Be Useful to You.*

6. How can teens carve out their own identity when they are also fighting the urge to fit in?
This question was definitely my struggle throughout high school. I would (and still do, to some extent) avoid talking about speeches and traveling because I didn't want to isolate myself from other kids by talking about a bunch of experiences that we hadn't shared. I sought to have more of the experiences that it felt like everyone had—the school dances, the pep assemblies, that kind of thing. In retrospect, though, fitting in with a group whose ideals you don't share is super overrated.

It's human nature to want to fit in with a group—that's a given. But if you're dissatisfied with the groups around you and you feel like you have to change who you are to fit in with them, don't try. Make your own group. And you'll belong there—because you made it. Organize an event, plan a concert, form a club, whatever. At my school we recently approved students' request to make a group called Warhammer 40K. Have I ever heard of this game? Nope. Do I think it's awesome that a bunch of kids who share this obscure interest are getting together to play? Hell yeah. Believe me, if you have an interest, there are other people out there with it too. For me, that place was called TEDxRedmond (the conference for youth I organized with a committee of all teenagers every year throughout high school).

7. How has having a passion impacted your teen years?
It's made me believe a lot more in sincerity and idealism, and in that sense I think it's made me less lazy. Sure, I still sleep in until eleven some weekends, but the point is that I feel like I have something to jump out of bed for. Isn't that what everyone wants for their life? It's made me ask more questions about why I do things, chase goals harder, and demand more from the things I do. Honestly, once you know what it's like to work for something because you're passionate about it, it's hard to go back to doing anything without passion—and I think that setting that bar is a good thing.

IF YOU WORK HARD FOR LITTLE GAIN?

What if you study hard and don't make great grades? Maybe you have a difficult time taking tests? Or have a hard time focusing in a quiet classroom? Maybe you're better at interactive learning. All of these reasons and many more can make school extremely frustrating. If this is the case, try talking to your parents and teachers about these issues. You do not have to struggle with this alone. They may be able to make some modifications that suit your learning style. No two people learn in the same way, and the goal is to find what works best for you. Don't let a bad grade change your future. There are many different ways to get where you're going, so don't give up on a dream because of grades.

Here's an example of exploring options to go after a dream: You want to be a chef. You love to cook for your family and friends, and you dream of owning your own restaurant someday. Unfortunately, you're not doing so hot in high school and are worried about getting into culinary school. Your favorite teacher recommends you get a part-time job in a restaurant and find a mentor. Once you start working at the restaurant, you start talking to the chefs and realize half of them went to culinary school, while the other half apprenticed as a chef with someone. Whenever you have an opportunity, you use your school projects to learn new things about the industry. Just last week you wrote a paper on Mexican cuisine for your Spanish class. You've learned that as long as you work hard, you will be able to pursue your dream of becoming a chef.

Stumbling through school bored and uninspired. *School is a huge waste of time.*

Spotlight
Katie Stagliano, Founder, Katie's Krops

Have you ever felt like school projects are a lot of work and a waste of time? How would you feel if you could get a great project grade, help more than two hundred people, and find something you are passionate about? That's exactly what happened to Katie in 2008 when she planted a cabbage seed in her backyard for a third-grade project. Her little seed grew to over forty pounds, so she donated it to a local soup kitchen, where it helped feed over 275 people.

When she realized what an impact her little garden made, she decided to plant even more produce. She asked her school to start a garden, and area farms to help in her efforts to feed the hungry. Now she has kids nationwide planting gardens to help out. Her goal is for every state to have at least one garden where 100 percent of the harvest is used to feed others. Every year she offers grants to individuals or groups ages nine to sixteen who are interested in planting a garden. To become part of Katie's gardening family, go to katieskrops.com. By igniting her spark, Katie has helped to feed thousands of people!

TAKE RESPONSIBILITY FOR YOUR EDUCATION

When it comes to your education, grab the reins and take charge. Your parents and teachers shouldn't have to force you to learn. Use the same amount of enthusiasm for your education that you have for your hobbies. Take advantage of this time in your life to explore your options and learn new things. You will only benefit from giving everything your best.

Make it your goal to find meaning in your work. This will make you more satisfied with school and a better student. Five years from now, you won't remember how you did on an algebra test, but you will remember the projects and assignments that helped you grow as a person. Every single one of those assignments can get you one step closer to igniting your spark.

No motivation. *All I care about is getting by without my teachers or parents on my back.*

Ignite Your Life Activity

Pick an activity you enjoy, or something new that stirs your curiosity. This can be a sport, club, environmental cause, game, or absolutely anything! Figure out a way you can merge that interest with projects or reports you may have in upcoming classes. See if you can figure out a way to integrate it with your language arts, science, and social studies classes. For example, if your interest is gaming, you could write an essay for language arts class comparing various forms of disruptive technology and how they have evolved over the years. For science class, you could dig into how gaming is helping to solve science problems. A social studies project may have you comparing various game companies or designers throughout history, or writing a case study on someone who has been influential. It's amazing how you can tie your interest into almost any school subject. If you approach your assignments with this mind-set, then you will enjoy them so much more, because you'll be able to apply what you learn to what you love to do!

6

SPARK UP YOUR ACTIVITIES

I want to have fun. It's a beautiful life.
You learn, you win, you lose, but you get up.
—Nas, Performer

ANYWHERE HIGH SCHOOL

At the end of each day, Jordan and his friends always meet at his locker to discuss after-school plans. The four of them have spent the last two months creating a YouTube channel with funny homemade videos and are trying to get viewers to their site.

Mark is the first to arrive. "We're not working on the site again today, are we?" he asks. "We should pick something else to do before Meredith and Jennie get here."

"What are you saying about us?" Jennie asks as she and Meredith join them at Jordan's locker.

"Our YouTube channel totally sucks. We only have twenty subscribers, and we spend all of our time working on it," Mark says.

Jordan rolls his eyes while Jennie nods her head in agreement with Mark.

"I'm not quitting," Meredith says. "We knew it would take a while to build up when we started this project."

"I agree with Mark," says Jennie. "I think we should do something else. What do you think, Jordan?"

"I knew it wouldn't catch on right away, but I think our stuff's funny. I'm going to keep putting videos up until people discover us. Eventually, we'll have our fan base."

FiND AN ACTIVITY YOU LOVE

What do you like to do in your spare time when you're not in school, spending time with your family, or hanging out with friends? Are you running from activity to activity because you have so many interests and are overcommitted? Maybe you've found the perfect balance between school, activities, and family time. Or are you still struggling to find your niche and plan your days? If your passions don't fall into the traditional school, sports, or after-school activities, then you may have to work a little harder to find something that sparks your interest. Get on your computer and do a search for *hobby* or *activity ideas* and you will get more results than you can imagine. Don't worry about whether you'll find other people interested in participating with you. Chances are that if you're interested in something, then someone else out there is too. So go ahead and ignite your after-school time with a brand-new activity!

Discover a new passion. *I'm going to try a painting class because I think it would be cool to create my own artwork for my room.*

Choosing Your Activity

If you don't already have an activity that you participate in, or if you're looking for a new one, it's important to find one that makes you excited. Ask yourself what you want to do and why you want to do it. Activities are time-consuming and require a commitment, so make sure you're doing them for the right reasons. Are you picking the activity only because your friends or parents want you to join? Or because it will look good on your transcripts? Sometimes this forces you to try something new and you end up loving the activity. Or it may turn out to be a short-term thing as you continue searching for that perfect hobby you will enjoy for many years. Here are a few you may want to consider:

Allowing someone else to choose your activities. *My dad and brother played football, so I play football.*

* Archery
* Blogging
* Building houses for Habitat for Humanity
* Computer programming
* Cooking
* Darts
* Frisbee golf
* Furniture painting
* Geocaching
* Inventing
* Photography
* Rock climbing
* Skeet shooting
* Yoga
* Running 5Ks
* Fishing
* Gardening
* Chess
* *YouTube* tutorials
* Collecting
* Woodworking

Spark Quiz
Help! I Don't Know Where to Look

Are you ready to find your perfect activity? After working hard at school all day, find something you really love to do. Activities are your chance to let loose and have a ton of fun. With an endless amount of options available, it can be tough to narrow them down. Take this short quiz to see where to start looking.

1. Your favorite class at school is
   a. Gym
   b. Speech
   c. Social Studies
   d. English
2. The event you would most like to attend is a
   a. Professional sporting event
   b. Broadway show
   c. Celebrity fundraiser
   d. High-profile court case
3. You love when you can
   a. Work as a team
   b. Have all eyes on you
   c. Rally for a cause
   d. Unleash your creativity
4. In your free time, you prefer to
   a. Shoot hoops
   b. Dance to your favorite songs
   c. Watch documentaries
   d. Blog

5. What television station are you most likely to watch?
   a. ESPN
   b. MTV
   c. Discovery
   d. Anything on my computer
6. What matters most for your new activity?
   a. Getting my body moving
   b. Recognition
   c. Helping other people
   d. Having a voice
7. If you won the lottery, what would you do?
   a. Set up a home gym
   b. Get private lessons in singing, dancing, and acting
   c. Set up a nonprofit
   d. Travel the world after graduation
8. What do you and your friends like to do in the summer?
   a. Swim, run, and play soccer
   b. Create YouTube videos
   c. Find somewhere to volunteer
   d. Write an e-zine, blog, or digital book
9. What do you find the most inspiring?
   a. The tricks and flips you see on the X Games
   b. Watching the show *American Idol*
   c. A rags-to-riches story
   d. When a first-time author hits the *New York Times* bestsellers list
10. What personality trait do you most admire?
    a. Competitiveness
    b. Imagination

    c. Passion

    d. Curiosity

Add up all of your *a*, *b*, *c*, and *d* answers. If you answered mostly *a*, then you like to be athletic. You like to keep your body moving and are up for burning off a little energy after school. Intramural sports are a great way to be a part of a team and represent your school. Your county recreation center, YMCA, or neighborhood should offer additional sports for your participation. If team sports aren't your thing, you can still be physical by playing tennis or golf, practicing yoga, or swimming laps.

Are your answers mostly *b*? Then you may have a flair for the dramatic. This can include acting, making music, dancing, or public speaking. You love to be onstage and feed off the energy of an audience. Your school should have a drama and music department, along with a debate team. Locally, your community may offer classes and productions you can join to explore your interest in the performing arts.

If you answered mostly *c*, then you are a helper. Try volunteer work or getting involved with a charitable organization. At school you can look into becoming a teen mentor or tutor. Your school may have clubs dedicated to fundraising, service projects, or helping your community. Is there a law you'd like to change or get passed to improve your community, help the environment, or aid teens? Then go online and see what other teens are doing to get support for their causes.

If you answered mostly *d*, then you are a curious person. You like to learn about new things and dig in for more information. Your school probably has a school newspaper where you can research and write stories. Online you can contribute articles to blogs like *HuffPost Teen*. Almost any organization would love to have someone who is interested in research, writing, or filming. You may find your calling is behind a camera, so you can look into activities for photography or moviemaking.

Illuminator: Beth Reekles, Author

How do you go from being a fifteen-year-old writing stories in your bedroom to being offered a three-book deal from Random House? If you're Beth Reekles, you post your novel on story-sharing website Wattpad and wait until it's viewed over 19 million times. This placed Reekles on *Time* magazine's "The 16 Most Influential Teens of 2013" list alongside people like Lorde, Hailee Steinfeld, and Malia Obama. Now she is a physics major at the University of Exeter in the United Kingdom, an author of three books, and a TEDxTeen Conference speaker. Find out more about Beth by visiting her at bethreekles.co.uk. Read on to learn how she used the internet to connect with other people, share her passion, and get noticed.

1. How did your interest in writing help you to connect with other people your age?

I actually used to think writing was a weird hobby because I didn't have any friends who wrote. When I found Wattpad, the online writing forum where I began posting my stories, I realized there were so many other teens who, like me, enjoyed writing and posting their work online—so I started to upload some of my own work. It was comforting to know there were other people my age who loved to write and it wasn't something to be laughed at for.

2. What advice can you give someone who wants to be a writer?

I'd definitely recommend looking at writing forums like Wattpad where you can self-publish easily and quickly, and get feedback on your work. I never thought I was any good at writing—it was just something I did for fun—so when I posted online and realized people actually liked my work, it was a huge confidence boost. I think posting your work online is a great starting place, especially for young people, because the communities on websites like Wattpad are really supportive.

3. Where did you get your confidence to post your first story?

I had pretty much zero confidence with my writing, but after I'd been reading on Wattpad for a while and had seen there were all these other people my age who were writing and putting their work out there, I remember thinking, *Why not? What have I got to lose?* After all, nobody on the site knew me, so they'd only judge my book by what they read. They wouldn't tell me my book was good just because they were my friends and being polite. The anonymity of it was a big appeal for me.

4. What advice can you give teens who are trying to find their passion?

I think it's important to try things and not be too concerned by what other people think—if you want to write, then write; if you want to play hockey, even if none of your friends do, do it. Do what makes you happy. If I'd stopped writing just because my friends didn't write and thought it was unusual, then I certainly wouldn't have gotten a three-book deal at the age of seventeen!

5. What should they do once they identify their dream?

Perseverance is key: I remember looking into publishing the year before I was offered my book deal with Random House, and the whole publishing industry looked so intimidating, I thought I would just be rejected because of my age if I tried to send my book to anybody, but that didn't stop me from self-publishing my work online. It's also important to find an outlet to share that dream—for example, lots of people who love singing post videos on YouTube.

6. How has having a passion helped you to discover who you are?
Being able to embrace my passion for writing has really helped me to become more determined and more confident. It's led to some incredible experiences—doing TV, radio, and newspaper interviews, for instance. And being seen as a role model to so many young girls has given me a greater sense of responsibility too.

WHERE DO VOLUNTEER WORK AND HAVING A JOB FIT IN?

You may be looking at your schedule and wondering where you can squeeze in an activity if you are doing volunteer work or have a job. Actually, they both count as activities. Some people prefer to spend their time helping other people or supporting a charitable cause. Or you may be someone who needs to make a little extra cash. Jobs, volunteer work, and internships give you real-world experience and a glimpse of the outside world. No matter which one you choose, you will learn valuable lessons in time management, responsibility, and working with other people. Warning: It's tempting to work as many hours as you can or to get wrapped up in a volunteer project. Make sure you are managing your time so you get enough sleep, have enough time to study, and can spend time with your friends and family too.

Gain valuable experience. *My job will teach me how to work with new people, work a cash register, and budget my money.*

COLLEGE APPLICATIONS AND ACTIVITIES

Do you need another excuse to be active? Extracurricular activities, volunteer work, and part-time jobs look awesome on college applications.

Colleges and universities aren't just looking for good grades anymore. They are looking for well-rounded individuals to attend their schools.

Activities don't have to be academic to look impressive on your application. If your transcript shows you did volunteer work at a hospital and started an archery club, then admission committees will assume you are compassionate, competitive, and organized. These differentiators might give you an edge when applying to your favorite schools. Don't choose activities just because you think they will look good on your transcripts, though. Pick activities that show who you really are. This way you can enjoy what you're doing while you're beefing up your resumé!

Try new things. *Interning at the radio station will show me what happens behind the scenes of a radio show.*

Illuminator: Lulu Cerone, Founder of LemonAID Warriors

When Lulu Cerone was in fifth grade, she organized a girls-versus-boys lemonade stand challenge to raise money for Haitian earthquake victims and then clean drinking water in Africa. The kids had a blast, and they raised a ton of money for charity. This launched the first of many PhilanthroParties. Now at sixteen years old, Lulu has helped over 4.2 million people organize their own events through her organization LemonAID Warriors. Her social activism has earned her a lot of support and recognition, like being named a 2014 Nickelodeon HALO honoree, receiving the Gloria Barron Prize for Young Heroes, winning the Montage Memory Makers Contest for humanitarians, and earning the President's Volunteer Service Award. To get more information about LemonAID Warriors, or to get to know Lulu, visit her website at lemonaidwarriors.com. Read on to learn how you can throw your own PhilanthroParty.

1. What inspired you to start LemonAID Warriors?

I was inspired to start LemonAID Warriors after the success of a fifth-grade boys-versus-girls LemonAID War I organized [to raise money] for the Haitian earthquake victims. I was shocked at the amazing impact of this simple event where we ended up raising $4,000. The real inspiration came when my friends begged me to organize more events because they had so much fun. I started to plan social activities with charitable themes and called them PhilanthroParties. I realized that showing compassion toward those in need actually made us kinder and more compassionate toward each other. These were bonding and empowering experiences, so LemonAID Warriors became a platform to share ideas that make social activism a part of our social lives.

2. What advice would you give teens who are trying to find their passion?

To find your passion, start off with identifying an activity that you truly love to do. The best chance you have of making a positive impact on the world is by committing to something fully for an extended period of time, and that's so much easier if you love what you do. Eventually, if you think creatively, you can find a way to turn that activity or skill into a tool for change. Maybe it's music or sports. Maybe it's shopping or playing video games. LemonAID Warriors has ideas to turn any passion into action.

3. What would you say to teens who feel the need to conform to their peers instead of expressing their uniqueness?

If you really feel the need to conform at the expense of expressing your uniqueness, then I would actually support that decision! Go ahead. Conform! It won't last long. Expressing uniqueness takes courage, and if you are not feeling confident enough just yet, then don't beat yourself up. Not everyone is born with confidence. Some of us need a little time. As long as you know and value what makes you unique, and as long as you keep developing your uniqueness, you will eventually have the confidence to express it and truly be yourself.

4. What's the greatest thing you've learned about yourself since starting LemonAID Warriors?
I learned that simple actions done with integrity and commitment have a powerful impact and create a ripple effect of positive change beyond what we can imagine.

5. How can teens become LemonAID Warriors?
Contact me on my website. Hopefully someday you can buy my book! Take advice from this interview. Throw a PhilanthroParty or put a charitable twist on something you already love doing. Keep it simple. Share your stories and photos with me, and I'll share them with my network to inspire others.

6. What's next for you?
I'd like to write a book to introduce some of these ideas and action plans that re-brand generosity and service ideas. Most people think of community service as a big project that is really hard to fit into your busy schedule. My ideas take [activities] you are already doing and give them a simple twist to turn them into tools for local and global change. Then I'd love to figure out how to get these ideas into schools. My personal passion causes have to do with basic human needs like water and education. I'm excited to continue developing creative ways to support these causes.

HELP! I'VE BEEN REJECTED

If you are going to try new things, meet new people, or challenge yourself, then you have to change your perception of rejection. You may have to face this when you invite someone to a dance, try out for a sports team, run for class office, interview for a part-time job, or in a million other possible scenarios.

You have nothing to lose by trying new things (like the above examples). The worst answer you can get is no; but you can't ever get a yes without taking that risk. If you run into an obstacle or roadblock, then try taking another route. If you lose your school election for student government, then con-

Letting your fear of rejection keep you from trying new things. *I'm not trying out for the team since I probably won't make it anyway.*

sider volunteering to help a local politician's campaign or join your school's debate team. There's always another way to participate in what you enjoy doing.

Spotlight
Austin Hay, Tiny House Builder

While many of his fellow high schoolers were hanging out with friends, playing video games, and thinking about graduation, Austin Hay was figuring out how to eliminate a future home loan. After his family home burned down and his dad had to rebuild it, Austin decided to start his own home-building project. With $2,000, he bought a trailer and began construction of his 130-square-foot house. Since he had no building experience, he needed to educate himself along the way.

His house took his entire high school career to build and ended up costing $12,000 to complete. It has electricity, a composting toilet, a shower, a refrigerator, and a cooktop. He sleeps in an upstairs loft. The tiny home is registered as a trailer, so he can drive it to college. You can watch a video tour of his home by visiting YouTube and entering his name. His amazing project has been featured on several news sources and blogs. By igniting his spark, Austin has managed to find a way to live on his own without having to pay rent or take out a home loan!

ACTIVITIES AND YOUR WELL-BEING

From the time you are born, life is a balancing act. Every day is a combination of obligations, self-care, and hopefully fun. Your sense of well-being counts on you to provide for your social, emotional, and spiritual needs. Activities are a great way for you to fulfill those needs with positivity.

Your social needs can be met when you're bonding with people who share your interests. Even if it's a solitary activity like writing or computer coding, you can join clubs or participate in online forums where you can discuss your activities.

Did you know that activities fulfill emotional needs? They give you all of those feel-good emotions like satisfaction, pride, and happiness. These positive emotions increase your self-confidence and make challenges easier to handle.

You might not consider your favorite activity spiritual if it's not affiliated with a religious institution, but spirituality can be found when you find a calling larger than yourself. If you do volunteer work, raise money for charity, or watch out for your younger siblings, then you are filling your spiritual cup.

Lacking balance between activities, school, and family time. *I'm too busy to have hobbies.*

Activities provide the perfect balance between what you need to do every day and what you want to do every day. They increase your sense of well-being and are a whole lot of fun. Some of the activities you try today may end up being lifelong hobbies or stepping-stones to your dream career. So get out there and try new things!

Ignite Your Life Activity

Think of something that interests you or that you'd like to learn more about, whether it's chemistry, coding, soccer, cooking, or painting. It can be anything. Now come up with an action plan on how you are going to pursue this activity. First, find an expert or mentor for this activity. This can be a coach or teacher at your school, or someone who has a string of YouTube videos providing instructions for your new activity. Think of some peers who already participate in this activity or may be interested in joining you. The goal is for you to build your own activity group consisting of an expert and of people your own age. For example, if you are interested in running a 5K race, you can contact your local running stores, the YMCA, and your school's cross-country team to gather information. The goal is to put your plan into motion.

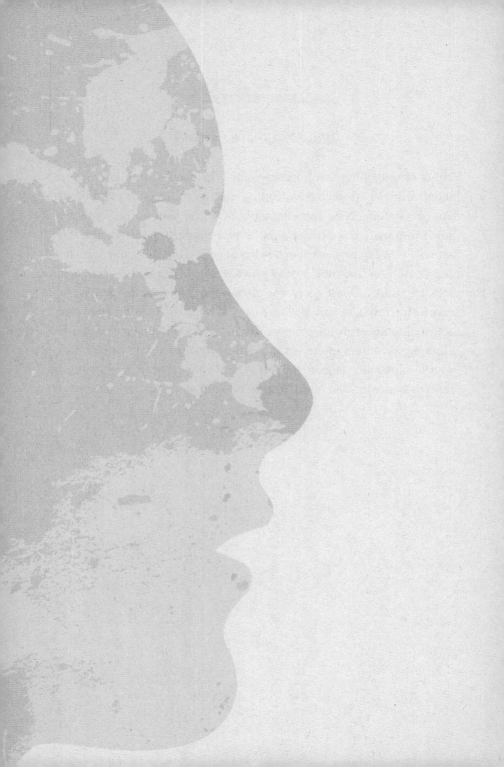

7

IGNITE YOUR DREAMS

A dream doesn't become reality through magic; it takes sweat, determination and hard work.
—*Colin Powell, Former Secretary of State*

ANYWHERE HIGH SCHOOL

Brad is lying on a blanket with India staring at the stars. "What are you going to do when we graduate from high school?" he asks.

"I'm going to college to study biology," India says. "Maybe I'll even be a doctor someday. What about you?"

"I don't know what I want to do. I don't even know if I want to go to college."

"What do you love to do? What are you interested in?" India asks.

"I know I want to see what life is like outside this town," Brad says. "I'd love to see the world."

"You should start researching jobs where you can travel. I bet there's all kinds of things you can do."

"I guess I can google it and see what pops up. Maybe it will help me decide about college."

DREAM IN ALL SIZES

Dreams can be both big and small. They can require hard work and stamina, or seem effortless to obtain. That's what makes dreams so interesting. They have no rules. You can dream to be an engineer, a music producer, or a star in Cirque du Soleil. They can be simple and short-term like learning to drive a car or play a guitar. Your dreams

Doing a new project or task only when it's required. *I'm joining the debate team, but only because it will look good on my transcripts.*

may revolve around a career, an activity you wish to pursue, or the type of family life you want in the future. With a dream you have no limits but endless possibilities. They give you something to look forward to, a purpose, and a place to aim your focus. Dreams come in all shapes and sizes. They are the things that make you want to jump out of bed in the morning and get started

on your day. Dreams can take you around the world or be obtained in your own backyard. They are your dreams, so get creative!

WAYS TO MAKE YOUR DREAM COME TRUE

There are so many different ways to go after your dreams. Some people like to jump right in, while others like to plan it out. Whether you are starting today or waiting for tomorrow, there are things you can do right now to make your dreams come true.

Own It

No one else is you! You have to own who you are and what makes your dream different. Each person has their own combination of skills, creativity, and interests to guide them. Being unique is a gift. Appreciate being different. Don't pursue other people's dreams—go after your own.

Believe It

Before anyone else will believe in your dream, you have to believe in it. You have to be confident your dream is achievable. Set small goals and reward yourself when you achieve them.

Fear Not

Are you terrified to take a chance on something new? Are you scared of failing, or being rejected? Don't let the butterflies in your stomach take control. Face your fear and go after what you want. If it doesn't work out, you'll be happy you gave it your best shot.

> Leave your comfort zone behind. *I'm going to try new things and be open to new experiences.*

Have Fun

Dreams are supposed to be fun, so enjoy the ride. Not every dream or activity has to be earth-shattering or a lead-up to your future career. Dreams ignite us and keep us excited in our day-to-day lives.

IS IT JUST MY IMAGINATION?

Remember when you were little and played dress up? Or you'd pretend to be a doctor, a singer, or a superhero? You used your imagination all the time. It's powerful stuff and the foundation for everything. Think of all the things you might take for granted, like soccer balls, magazines, clothing, headphones, and even tacos. They were all created from someone's imagination. As a kid, tapping into your imagination was as natural as eating and breathing. As you get older, it's harder to do. Many people start thinking in terms of black and white. They see imagination and daydreaming as a waste of time.

What is imagination beyond pretend play and kids' games? It's when you close your eyes and picture something that doesn't exist. When you believe you can make the impossible a possibility. It's when you set goals and develop ways to reach them. It lets you stretch your mind and come up with new ideas.

When you act on your imagination, you tap into your creativity. Creativity is not just about the arts and performing. Look at Apple products like the iPad, iPhone, and MacBook. Steve Jobs, Apple's CEO, was one of the most creative geniuses of all time, and he was a computer guy! He had a vision for new technology and a way to present the products so people of all ages were interested. Every time Apple releases a new product, people are literally lined up outside the doors to buy it! Now that's some creative thinking!

Tap into your imagination. *I'm not going to limit myself on what I can do.*

Spark Quiz
You Must Be Dreaming

So you may be thinking, *I'd love to start working on my dream. I'd love to have a passion and something that makes me excited. So how do I find it?* For most people it does not come easy. Have you heard the expression, "You have to kiss a lot of frogs to find a prince"? Sometimes the same goes for finding things you love to do. You have to try a lot of new things to find the one thing that's special. Here's a personality quiz that can help you to narrow the options down.

1. In my dream job, I would
   a. Be changing the world.
   b. Travel and have lots of responsibility.

   c. Rule the world!

   d. Be adored by millions of people.

2. I'm best described as someone who
   a. Is always helping other people.
   b. Is up on all the current news. The internet is my life!
   c. Is the master of extracurricular activities.
   d. Loves to perform.

3. My best summer ever would be spent
   a. Building houses for Habitat for Humanity.
   b. Working two jobs and saving a ton of money.
   c. Interning for a CEO of a major company. I wouldn't mind fetching their coffee!
   d. Creating a YouTube channel with me as the star.

4. I like to hang out
   a. Wherever I am needed.
   b. With my friends, classmates, or coworkers.
   c. At organized events.
   d. On Twitter. Does that count?

5. I most look up to
   a. Oprah. She gives tons of money to help other people.
   b. Mark Zuckerberg. He started Facebook while he was still in college.
   c. The president. It's the most powerful job!
   d. Adam Levine and anyone on *The Voice*!

6. With clothes, I like to
   a. Make sure I'm comfortable and casual.
   b. Be accessorized from head to toe.
   c. Be crisp and very polished looking.
   d. Be the first person at school to start a new trend.

7. School is important because
   a. Not everyone is lucky enough to get an education.
   b. I need good grades to get into the college of my choice.
   c. Student council needs me!
   d. I get to see all of my friends.
8. The thing that would most likely brighten my day is
   a. Getting a thank-you card from someone I helped.
   b. Being asked to be the leader on a school project.
   c. Getting a standing ovation after my student council speech.
   d. Discovering my blog has a lot of new readers.

If you answered mostly *a*, then you are a helper! You appreciate life and enjoy helping other people. Many different activities and jobs fall into this category. You may enjoy volunteering your time to a worthwhile organization or fighting social injustices. Every industry needs people just like you to form human connections. Try getting involved in a charitable organization so you can start fulfilling your dream to make a difference in someone else's life.

If you answered mostly *b*, then you are an operator! You like to organize activities and make sure they are executed correctly. You enjoy the responsibility of a part-time job or being in charge of an extracurricular activity. You are focused and like to work on many different projects at one time. Your dream may be to be an event planner, project manager, or consultant. Look for activities where you can put your organizational skills to great use.

If you answered mostly *c*, then you are a leader! You may want to start working on your campaign speech now because your student council is looking for people just like you. Don't limit yourself to politics. Every activity needs someone who is good at bringing people together. By following your dreams, you will be in a position to inspire other people as well.

If you answered mostly *d*, then you are a performer! Whether it's onstage, on the internet, or as the class clown, you love an audience. We are a technology-driven world, so you may want to use your skills on social media. If you are creative, the arts offer a lot of different options. Whether your dream is to entertain, be a public speaker, or speak your mind, you will have opportunities to be center stage at every phase of your life.

Illuminator: Chip Hiden, *The Dream Share Project*

The Dream Share Project started with a map, a video camera, and the desire to interview people who were following their dreams. Chip Hiden and his partner Alexis Irvin had one goal: to empower and inspire young people to chase their dreams. They took a road trip with that mission in 2010, and since then, they have produced a documentary and written the book *Build Your Dreams: How to Make a Living Doing What You Love*. To be inspired by their interviews, visit thedreamshareproject .com. Read on to learn how they help people find their true purpose by hosting workshops all across the country.

1. How did your teen years help you to realize your dream?
When I was seventeen and about to graduate high school, I was diagnosed with diabetes. This seemingly negative experience was actually a catalyst for my first real passion project. A few friends and I decided

to fight back against diabetes by organizing the Chipapalooza Charity Concert in my backyard, which raised money for the Juvenile Diabetes Research Foundation. We invited local bands; borrowed a sound system; made T-shirts; organized games, prizes, raffles; and got a street team together for a big grassroots marketing campaign. The first event was a huge hit and a ton of fun, so we continued planning the annual event for six years, raising over $10,000, working with over thirty amazing bands, and even booking a minor league baseball stadium to host the event in our final year. The Chipapalooza experience was a crash course in business, event planning, activism, leadership, marketing, nonprofit management, and a ton of other skills that have proved invaluable over the years. Thanks to Chipapalooza, I was able to get a dream job in college planning huge all-campus concerts and comedy events. And after college, I felt prepared to take on the entrepreneurial challenge and risk of producing an independent film, *The Dream Share Project*.

I think the overall lesson here is that negative events in our lives can be transformed into positive action. Life throws us all sorts of curveballs and challenges—it's part of the human condition. The key is in how we respond to negativity. We all have a choice: be consumed by negativity or find a way to harness that fire, find a mission worth fighting for, and pursue a dream that fills life with a sense of purpose and meaning.

2. How did **The Dream Share Project** get started?

After college, Alexis and I both stuck to the traditional "safe" path and got office jobs despite the entrepreneurial spirit we both had. We needed to pay the bills, and there wasn't much of a choice. At first, the jobs were exciting. Even better, they paid well! However, we quickly realized we weren't cut out for the cubicle. So we started quietly hatching plans to take a grand adventure across the United States—to see the beauty of the country and to film interviews with people who loved their jobs. We set up thirty different interviews with entrepreneurs, activists, artists, athletes, inventors, and creative types. Our goal was to learn how these people figured out their passion and transformed it into a career that made them happy, paid the bills, and had a positive impact on their communities. Once we had the plan, we created a budget, saved every penny we could, and researched our trip for a year before we were able to turn in our two weeks' notice and hit the road.

3. What advice can you give teens who are trying to find their passion?
Start an independent project and bring it to life—it could be a website, a short video, a screenplay, a novel, a book proposal, a play, a song, a rock opera, a science application, a piece of art, a political campaign, a rally, an event, a fundraiser, a podcast, baked goods to sell, jewelry or clothing to sell, etc.

Pick something you're interested in, curious about, fired up about, or that just sounds fun. Don't settle for something your teacher assigns you, or that parents tell you to do, or that is only designed to beef up your resumé. Experience is the greatest teacher you will ever have, so don't sit back and wait for your lightbulb moment. Go out and get busy!

4. What should they do once they identify their dream?
Find a way to test-drive the dream to confirm that you enjoy that actual nitty-gritty work. Many people think that being a rock star is an awesome dream, but they may be singing a different tune after a day of practicing guitar for eight hours, fingers callused and aching, with a long way to go before mastering their favorite song. For others, there is no feeling sweeter than aching, callused fingers and the satisfaction of a long day's work toward something they intrinsically love. Either way, you need to experience the nitty-gritty before deciding to move forward or not.

You can test-drive your dream through independent study or practice, by joining a club or team, by volunteering, by seeking an internship or part-time job, by taking a class, or through job shadowing.

5. How does setting goals help you achieve your dreams?

Many people feel overwhelmed and paralyzed by how big their dream is. They have no idea how to get started. Having a plan and a list of mini-goals will help you stop worrying and get started. Don't worry too much about step ninety-nine of your plan. Instead, focus on step one. What is one small action you can take today to get a little bit closer to your dream? Get in the habit of asking yourself this each morning, and soon you will be making serious progress.

When setting goals, get as specific as possible and be sure to assign a deadline. For example, "Book a show for my band" is not as good of a goal as "Contact the manager of the Black Cat music venue at 2:00 PM on Thursday to ask if they will book band."

6. How can having a dream help a teen get through tough times?

During our travels with *The Dream Share Project*, we met an upbeat, energetic student named Hector Manley who had gone through some incredibly tough times. Hector lost both of his legs in a fire at age eleven. However, at age twenty-two, Hector became the first double ampu-tee to kayak the entire Mississippi River. In addition to rowing 2,500 miles in three months, Hector managed to raise nearly $50,000 for the Wheelchair Foundation and the Wounded Warrior Project. Hector told us his next goal is to climb Aconcagua, a twenty-three-thousand-foot mountain in South America. I still remember how Hector simply radi-ated with passion and zest for life. I've never been more convinced of the healing and rejuvenating power of dreams. When life gets tough, a dream gives you a reason to get up in the morning and work toward something greater than yourself.

7. If you could go back and give advice to your teen self, what would it be?

Do more nerdy things! Don't be afraid to try a ton of stuff that takes you out of your comfort zone, even if you think it makes you look nerdy or geeky. Nerds are inheriting the earth—the best of business, pop culture, science and medicine, and technology—it's all lovingly created by a bunch of hardworking nerds. Don't worry about appearances so much.

Also, I would tell my younger self to focus more on helping others and to practice more humility. I think in high school especially, there can be serious temptation to become self-focused and even self-centered. However, life's greatest moments come when we cast aside vanity, truly listen to the needs of others, and ask, "How can I help?"

8. *What's next for* **The Dream Share Project?**
We are currently filming two more documentaries and working on several book ideas. We're continuing to tour the country to share our film with college students, which is great because we both absolutely love to travel! Finally, we're developing a college and high school curriculum to accompany *The Dream Share Project* film and *Build Your Dreams* book.

WHAT IF NOTHING SPARKS YOUR INTEREST?

Take a moment and relax your body and mind. I want you to picture a moment when you were so involved with what you were doing that you lost track of time. What were you doing when this happened? How did it make you feel to be totally immersed? How can you replicate this feeling in the future? Take notice of the moments when you feel in your groove, and see if you can incorporate those activities into the dreams you have for yourself.

Does the thought of a traditional career make you want to yawn? Do you feel uninspired at school and a little lost when it comes to developing your interests? Don't worry! There's something out there for you. Everyone has their own special talents, and

Start a project. *I'm going to create a YouTube channel because I think it would be fun to record videos with my friends.*

some people have to search harder to find them, but it's definitely worth it. Take a look at this list of nontraditional careers. Do a search on the internet if any of them interest you.

Just think . . . the next time you eat a candy bar it may be for research!

* Air traffic reporter
* Biker photographer for Google Maps
* Chocolate taster
* Cirque du Soleil performer
* Cruise ship director
* English teacher in a foreign country
* Ethical hacker
* Food stylist
* Greeting card artist
* Makeup artist
* Teddy bear repair technician
* Tropical island caretaker
* Video game designer
* Volcanologist
* Waterslide tester

Illuminator: Emily Matson and Julianne Goldmark,
Entrepreneurs, Emi-Jay

When best friends Emily Matson and Julianne Goldmark were fourteen years old, they loved the hair accessories worn on their favorite television show, *Gossip Girl.* They just didn't like the prices when they tried to buy them for themselves, so they started making their own. Emily's mom told her friend, a celebrity hair stylist, what the girls were up to, and the next thing they knew, Jennifer Aniston was wearing one of their hair ties to a movie premiere. Since that memorable event, their hair accessories can be seen on A-listers of all ages. They have collaborated with Splendid and Spanx, and have been featured in *O, The Oprah Magazine*; *Marie Claire*; and *Seventeen* magazine. They donate 20 percent of their proceeds to charity and partner with the women's network Step Up's Young Luminaries program to promote self-confidence and education to girls worldwide. To check out their cool products or learn more about Emily and Julianne, visit emi-jay.com. Read on to find out how these full-time college students manage to run a multimillion-dollar company.

1. How did Emi-Jay get started?
EM: Emi-Jay began February of 2009 when Julianne and I began to notice a growing trend of hair accessories on TV shows and among our friends at school. However, most of the pieces on the market were too elaborate for everyday wear or far out of a teenager's price range. With that in mind, we went to the Los Angeles Fashion District and bought materials, went back to Julianne's house, and began experimenting with our findings. However, the business itself really launched when my mom's hair stylist, Chris McMillan, said he was looking for a sleek, bow-like hair tie. From there, Julianne and I whipped up something to fit his criteria, he put one on Jennifer Aniston to wear on the red carpet, and shortly thereafter we received an email from *Marie Claire* magazine asking to feature one of our hair ties. We had to come up with a company name, launch a website, and the rest is history!

2. Where did you learn to sew hair ties and create headbands?
JG: We actually never sewed our hair accessories at the beginning. We cut our fabric and created hair ties with simple steps rather than having to learn to sew or anything.

3. Do you have mentors and people you look up to?
EM: Absolutely! As young women, I think our moms have been both instrumental and incredibly influential throughout the entire process.

They are always there for us, and it's hard to imagine where we would be without their support. They allow us to run a business while simply being teenagers and living our lives.

4. What advice can you give a young person who wants to be an entrepreneur?
JG: Besides having confidence in your concepts and business ideas, I think it's really important to surround yourself with positive, supportive people. If I've learned to appreciate one thing, it's definitely the friends and family that have always been by my side through this experience.

5. How does setting goals help you?
EM: Goals are a way of making your dreams tangible. For me, personally, lists are an incredible way of getting myself closer to my goals. I love the fulfilling feeling of checking things off a piece of paper—it's validation that I'm actually getting things accomplished, even if it's step by step!

6. Where did you get the confidence to start a business at such a young age?
JG: It honestly came very naturally to us. It happened all organically, starting in my house, then moving into a small office, and now a big office space. The confidence grew as we saw that people loved that we were so young and creating products, while also giving back to our community.

7. What advice can you give teens who are trying to find their passion?
JG: Let it come naturally to you! Also, a lot of times people like to keep their work interests and hobbies separate, but I think if you can come across something that incorporates both, you'll be so passionate about it.

8. What should they do once they identify their dream?
EM: Be proactive and pursue it in any possible way. We're so lucky to live in a time where everything is so easily accessible through the internet.

Social media is also an incredible and free tool; it's a vehicle to showcase your passions, ideas, and talents to the entire world.

UNREALISTIC DREAMS?

What if your dream is to become a dancer, but you have two left feet? Or you love medicine, but the sight of blood makes you faint? Sometimes you may feel like your dreams are out of reach. How can you be a singer if you can't carry a tune? You may not become a dancer for the New York City Ballet, a doctor, or the next Pharrell, but these passions can lead you to greater things. If your interest is in singing or dancing, you may like production, casting, or directing. Someone with an interest in medicine might enjoy research, chemistry, or pharmacology. Explore all of the many interesting roles within the industry. You may just find the perfect fit.

Dreams can be fulfilled without being a career too. You can pursue your dreams through hobbies. Not everyone can be the next Beyoncé, but you can take dance classes, join a singing group, and enjoy them as activities. Hobbies are a great way to make friends, relieve stress, and have a great time. They give us a chance to express ourselves creatively and without judgment.

Negativity. *There's no way I could ever invent something cool.*

Spotlight
Flynn McGarry, Chef

What do Yorkshire pudding, sea urchin, and roasted pumpkin with bacon have in common? If you answered that they were all cooked in Flynn McGarry's bedroom, then you'd be correct. Instead of going for the typical teen decor of posters and video games, he decided to turn his bedroom into a kitchen. At the age of eleven, he started a monthly supper club called Eureka out of his house, where eight- to ten-course meals were served to as many as twenty people. His training early on came from cookbooks and online videos.

Now he can be found apprenticing at some of the hottest restaurants with the most talented chefs. When he comes up with a concept for a meal and is planning his menu, he draws a picture of how he will serve it. He likes to use his creativity to prepare a meal that is visually appetizing and delicious. Someday he would like to be the chef and owner of the best restaurant in the world. To see what Flynn's serving up for dinner, visit him at diningwithflynn.com. By igniting his spark, Flynn is well on his way to becoming a culinary superstar!

FINDING THOSE DREAMS

Tapping into your dreams and making plans for your future require a lot of self-awareness. They require you to know what makes you thrive as a person. These insights can lead you in the right direction when you go looking for your dreams. Start to ask yourself: What are my strengths and weaknesses? What motivates me? When am I the happiest?

Being close-minded about trying new things. *I've got enough going on and don't need to try something new.*

Dreams will give your life meaning and a purpose. You grow as a person when you are challenged and stretched to achieve something new. So even if your dream of becoming a comic book illustrator changes and you decide to become a landscaper instead, you will still benefit. The positive emotions of accomplishment, happiness, inspiration, and hope will stick with you no matter how many times your dreams change.

Ignite Your Life Activity

Kick-start your imagination by creating an inspiration collage on a bulletin board or on Pinterest. Look for pictures and quotations that say something about you. If you like music, cut out a picture of an instrument. If you are a programmer, then look for pictures of games and apps you think are cool. Anything that represents you! At first, you may feel like you have a random group of pictures, but the idea is to form connections between your different interests. For example, if you clip a picture of a comedian and a quotation about writing and you enjoy computers, you may enjoy starting a comic where you create funny characters. Look at your inspiration board to see if you can find some fun new activities!

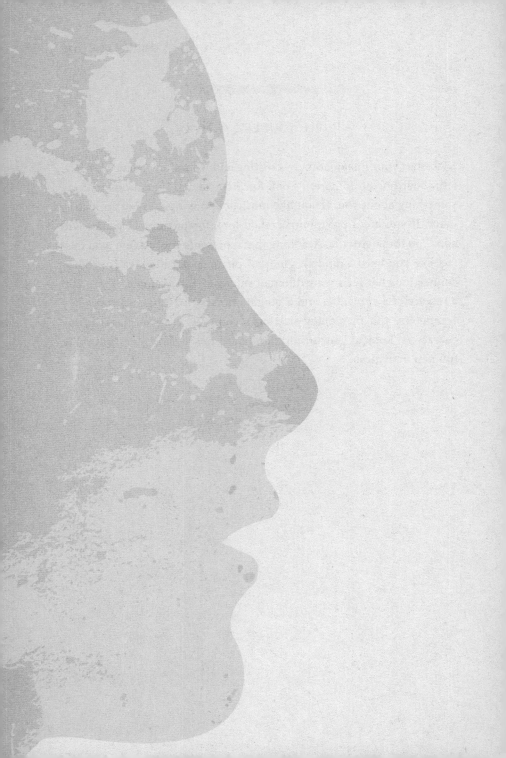

8

SPARK UP YOUR DETERMINATION

Grit is sticking with your future, day in, day out, not just for the
week, not just for the month, but for years, and working really
hard to make that future a reality.
—*Angela Lee Duckworth, PhD, Psychologist*

ANYWHERE HIGH SCHOOL

"I don't know if I'm going to audition this year," Taylor says. "I might
just sit this one out."

"Yeah right. You've been in every play since you came to this school,"
Arianna says.

"I'm serious. I'm sick of spending all my free time in rehearsals. It's
like having a full-time job. I'd actually like to have a social life this year.
Who cares about the school play anyway?" Taylor says while thumbing
through a series of text messages.

"You used to care before you started dating Sheila. Now all you do
is hang out with her."

"This isn't about her. I've got too much stuff going on with school
right now. I have to keep my grades up if I want to get into a good
college."

Arianna isn't buying it. "I hope she's worth it, because this is the last performance before graduation. It's pretty crappy that you're bailing on everyone."

Taylor walks away second-guessing the decision. Why did everything always have to be so complicated?

ARE YOU READY TO GO THE DISTANCE?

Not setting long-term goals. *I'm too young to worry about my future.*

Combine sprints and marathons in life. *I'll use half of my allowance as spending money and save the other half for a car.*

We have all heard the saying "Life is not a sprint; it's a marathon." Teachers and business leaders use this phrase all the time. But what does it really mean, and why should you care?

The purpose of a sprint is to go a short distance and get there quickly. A marathon, on the other hand, requires patience, endurance, and grit. Most people really like the sprints. It's fun to get immediate results. Marathons, on the other hand, take a lot of time and patience. Think of all the New Year's resolutions people make every year. Most of them don't stick. It's hard to sustain a high level of interest in something for a long period of time, especially if the payoff seems way into the future. Find ways to reward yourself along the way to maintain your enthusiasm, so you can obtain your end goals. Look at the following chart to see the difference between sprints and marathons.

Sprint vs. Marathon

Sprint	Marathon
Using your babysitting money from Monday to buy an iTunes card on Saturday	Saving money year after to year to buy a car
Studying for a science test	Studying in college for seven years to become a physical therapist
Dieting and exercising for a few weeks to look good for prom	Adopting a healthy diet and exercise plan to lead a healthy life
Writing an article for the school newspaper	Writing a book and going through the publishing process
Donating the books you've read to a charity	Organizing a book drive to create a library at a local group home

It's best to have both sprints and marathons in your life. With sprints, you reap the rewards of an accomplishment in a short period of time. For example, a blogger can post an article online and get feedback immediately. If that same blogger decides to write a book—a marathon—then they must wait during the writing and publishing process before they have a finished product, but the reward is ultimately higher than with the single blog post. In other words, the road to self-discovery and pursuing your dreams is going to take a little time and work. Are you up for the challenge? If so, get ready to pace yourself. You may run into roadblocks and obstacles, but your grit and determination will get you to the finish line.

Spark Quiz
Who Are You?

Before you start planning your sprints and marathons, it's important for you to get to know yourself. Setting long-term goals is a big deal, and you want to make sure you are focused on the ones that best fit your personality. Take this quiz to check your self-awareness. Don't be shocked if you have a hard time coming up with some of the answers.

1. Set a timer. How long does it take you to name the three things you spend the most time doing in a week?
   a. I'm still working on it.
   b. Five minutes.
   c. Less than a minute.
2. What would you say if a friend asked you to try a new activity with them?
   a. "I'll have to think about it."
   b. "It depends; what are we doing?"
   c. "Count me in!"
3. When do you feel thankful?
   a. Thanksgiving.
   b. When my friends give me birthday presents.
   c. Every day!
4. When clothing shopping, how do you pick out clothes?
   a. I look at items by size.
   b. I grab items in my size but in a few other sizes as well.
   c. I try things on based on my favorite colors and styles.
5. When you are planning to go to the movies with friends, how do you choose the movie?

     a. I make someone else choose.

     b. I offer an opinion on which movie to see.

     c. I pick the movie since I know what everyone likes.

6. Set a timer. How long does it take for you to think of three of your weaknesses?

     a. I'm still working on it.

     b. Five minutes.

     c. Less than a minute.

7. Can you quickly name three things you like to do?

     a. I need to think about this for a while.

     b. Maybe one or two things.

     c. Definitely.

8. Do you know what you want to be when you get older?

     a. I'll figure it out eventually.

     b. I have a few ideas.

     c. Of course!

If you answered mostly *a*, then it's time to get to know yourself. It's one of the most important things you will ever do. Throughout this book, you are learning tips and tricks on how to discover and develop your true self. Come back to this quiz often to see if your answers change over time.

If you answered mostly *b*, then you are halfway down the path to self-discovery. You've started to discover some things you like to do and are open to new ideas. Make sure you are doing the activities in this book. They help you to expand your ideas and learn more about your true self.

If you've answered mostly *c*, congratulations! You've got a great grasp on who you are, and you aren't afraid to express your opinions. You're ready to take the next step by setting some short-term and long-term goals.

Illuminator: Krystyn Lambert, Magician

What do you do if you love to act, have a head for logic, and enjoy science fiction? If you are Krystyn Lambert, you become a magician! Lambert became a pro at the age of twelve when she was admitted as the youngest member of the Junior Society at the famous Magic Castle. In 2010 her feature in the award-winning documentary *Make Believe* opened the door for her to become a popular motivational speaker at schools all over the world. By 2012 she was asked to be the closing speaker at the TEDxTeen Conference and was named by *Teen Vogue* as one of the "Four Youth Activists to Watch from TEDxTeen." She starred in Criss Angel's *BeLIEve* television show and is an honors student at the University of California, Los Angeles. Visit krystynlambert.com to find out where you can catch one of her magical shows! Read on to learn how Krystyn used magic to increase her self-confidence and build a career.

1. How did knowing you had a passion for magic help you through your teen years?
My friends joke that magic is my boyfriend. It's all I talk about, and it's all I spend time doing. I started practicing magic when I was nine, and started to take it seriously, making it more than a hobby, when I was twelve years old.

In other words, magic gave me something to live for. I was opinionated, assertive, and disinterested in things most of my peers were into. Basically, I didn't have a whole lot of friends. But I had magic. I could devote all my energy to it, disappearing into hours of contemplation and practice. No matter what mean kids said at school and no matter how lonely I felt, it was always there for me. But it was sort of a catch-22.

Magic gave me a respite from being a social dud, but it also sort of perpetuated it. I mean it's not like basketball practice. Someone can say, "Man, I spent three hours yesterday working on my free throw," and even though I know virtually nothing about basketball, I can still roughly understand how those three hours were spent. With magic, I can't say, "Man, I spent three hours yesterday working on this false shuffle," because well, for one, I can't tell you that a thing called a false shuffle exists because it's a "secret magic move." So there's certain alienation inherent in magic.

Regardless of any social duress it may have caused, magic wound up helping me stay on track. It gave me a sense of a higher purpose. Not only was it a creative and productive outlet, but also when I started doing real shows, I realized there was a world outside of high school. I wasn't limited to math tests and wondering whom I could sit with at lunch. There was a bigger agenda on my plate. I would perform anywhere and everywhere. It didn't matter to me—I'd perform at schools, birthdays, dinner parties, small theaters, or restaurants. By the time I finished high school, I'd accumulated a substantial resumé and started to travel internationally, taking acts to Europe, Asia, and South America. I competed in magic competitions, winning the title of World Teen Magician, and became the subject of a documentary, *Make Believe*.

I started to learn that Sarah sneering at me when I gave a passionate answer in English class didn't matter. I won't say that it didn't sting, but it stung far less, because I had the knowledge she was essentially irrelevant to my path in life. It's so easy to get caught up in the drama of high school: popularity, bullying, and teachers' pets. But with my mind set on magic, I was able to better keep my eye on my own prize. I focused on what my goals were and why I wanted to achieve them. This helped me to overcome all the nonsense that accompanies teen life.

2. Where did you get your confidence to start performing at such a young age?

I think performance is in my blood. My mother was pregnant with me while she was in *Guys and Dolls*, and I feel a part of me never got off the stage. When I was two years old, I wandered off at the mall; security and my very panicked mother eventually found me posing in front of a five-way mirror. I was promptly put into dance classes. From there, I would go on to spend the next ten years prancing around for a crowd of senior citizens as I starred in a long list of adapted children's musicals.

Performance was never a choice for me; it was something I *had* to do. And I don't mean I was forced by outside sources. Not at all. It was pure emotional necessity. Performance is a blood sport. You don't think of it that way when you approach it purely intellectually, but ultimately it's a task of guts. You've got to be alive and on highest alert, connecting with a room full of people tracing your every move. It's live. It's raw; there's no editing, no masks even if you are playing a character. Performance is just you and your bare soul.

But as I grew more aware of others around me—the inevitable peers who like to snicker—there were times when I got nervous. What if I wasn't good enough? What if my act wasn't rehearsed enough? What if people thought I looked stupid? These are all perfectly legitimate feelings. However, when all is said and done, I had to trust myself. I was onstage for a reason, and I had to own that. I had to own what I was doing, who I was, and why I was there.

As far as difficult people are concerned, I can't control every audience member's feelings, but I can control my own. No matter what I do, some people might not like it; some people might be having a bad day. I can't let that affect me. I have my own journey to contend with, and that's plenty enough. I believe in what I'm doing and where I'm going, but I can't expect everyone else to. To this day, I have to keep this in perspective. I have to know in my heart that I deserve to be where I am and that I can't let anyone stand in my way. This takes a lot of courage, and it's not always easy. I can still see the faces of certain girls from my high school class glaring at me or laughing when I tried my hardest, and there are some days when this is hard to overcome. But when push comes to shove, they're not doing what I'm doing. They're not in my shoes. It's much harder to build something than it is to tear it down. At the end of the day, frivolous criticism is not pertinent to me or what I'm out to do.

The bottom line is that you're smart enough, clever enough, talented enough, and awesome enough. Deep down, you *know* you are; it's the plain and simple truth. So you just get out there and do your thing like it's nobody's business.

3. What advice can you give teens who are trying to find their passion?
The most important aspect of finding your passion, to me, is honesty. You can't let anyone tell you what you should or shouldn't be passionate about. No one can say, "Be excited about this or that." It has to come naturally. People typically become successful in their fields because they care about what they're doing. The best scientists are those who are passionate about what they're studying; the best teachers care about helping people learn. The passion has to be genuine. Be real with yourself, and find what truly suits you, not just what is "supposed to."

So how do you find this burning passion? You have to be active and try new things. Explore everything you can; step out on a limb and risk feeling uncomfortable. You can't be closed off to things, definitively saying that it's not for you. As annoying as the old adage "You never know unless you try!" is, it's really true. So check out a book about astronomy or take a pottery class. If it doesn't work out, who cares? You've learned that much more about yourself. And what didn't work out might lead you to something else; or maybe the one thing that was cool about that experience could turn into something way bigger. You never know.

You've got to stay thirsty for what might intrigue you. Keep your ears perked for something interesting that might come your way. The world is crazy; weird stuff is happening all the time if we keep on the lookout for it. The way you observe the world is different than how everybody else does, and that makes your view special. Your unique take on things is what you have to pay attention to, because therein lies the key.

Do you remember the first thing that ever blew your mind? Maybe it was volcanoes, dinosaurs, or outer space? And what was it that piqued your interest? These things give us a cause to wonder and push us to expand our minds more. Learn as much as you can about as much as you can. Keep track of your thoughts and feelings about things, and listen to what emerges. Just keep going, and your naturally curious and creative self will take flight.

4. What should you do once you identify your dream?

You've got to trust you're doing the right thing for yourself, and then believe in yourself. There's a Henry Ford quote that comes to mind, "Whether you believe you can do a thing or not, you are right." And believing one way or the other is your choice, not anyone else's. However, sometimes when I hear people vacuously telling me to believe in my dreams, I get frustrated. This is because simple belief will only take you so far. You have to take the plunge and start working.

You've probably heard the saying "Take life one day at a time," but I prefer the twenty-minute rule. I take things twenty minutes at a time. Maybe twenty-five. It's easy to get ahead of yourself or to feel overwhelmed by all you want to accomplish. By planning things out in twenty-minute increments, I find that I don't get the feeling of, *I don't even know where to begin!* Create a game plan and start plugging away. Even if your initial efforts don't wind up being applicable in the long run, they help get your feet wet. They get you in motion, and that first step is the most important.

What should the first step be? The most straightforward one I can think of is to start developing the most comprehensive knowledge of the field as possible. Whether it's a sport or an instrument, learn everything you can about it. Read about the history, new techniques, and even other subjects that are only tangentially related. Get it marinating in your brain, allowing yourself to be obsessed. Let your passion take you on a ride. And then practice, practice, practice. Soccer, debate, acting, horseback riding, or a new business venture, all require time, dedication, and patience. Rome wasn't built in a day. Think of yourself as a marble sculpture. It takes effort to nurture the marble into its full form. Be nice to yourself and continue to love what you're doing first and foremost. Everything else follows.

Once you start taking something seriously and putting in a lot of energy, there's this little bug that creeps in your ear. Let's call him Self-Doubt. And he reminds me of a possible outcome for my efforts, one of the scariest things in the world, at least to me: failure. I'm such a perfectionist, my fear of failing can be crippling. Fear of failure is probably the least productive human motivation, largely because it hinders your growth. Success is a sign you're ready to learn something new, and failure is a sign you're learning something new. You can't always succeed your first time, but you can fail less each time you try. By becoming friends with failure, you start to free yourself of the oppressive critic inside who won't let you be the best you.

5. Where do you see yourself in ten years?
When I perform magic, the response I get is surprise and intrigue. And not just from the demonstration I'm performing. I challenge people's association of a woman's role typically being that of an assistant, not a magician. Additionally, my acts aren't your average magic show . . . And they're certainly not what you'd expect from a pretty, blond girl. The Barbies of the world tend not to walk on glass or eat razor blades.

My dream is to have my own touring show. I want to become the most substantial woman in magic and help to inspire a culture where girls feel empowered to pursue their passions, whatever they are.

WHAT IS GRIT AND WHY DOES IT MATTER?

Do you ever look at your student class president, your school valedictorian, a team captain, or a classmate with a cool part-time job and wonder, *Why are they so lucky?* According to psychologist Dr. Angela Lee Duckworth, luck is not why most people succeed.[1] Success is not

Don't be afraid to get gritty. Even though I have a hard time with algebra, I'm going to keep studying it until I've got it figured out.

tied to having the highest test scores, being blessed with good looks, or having a certain amount of money in your family's bank account. When it comes down to it, success may be predicted by how much grit you have. What's grit? Grit is pursuing your goal over a long period of time and sticking with it even when things get hard. Grit is falling off a skateboard and getting back on again. Grit's about practicing the same piano solo over and over again until you get it right. Grit is researching computer programming and teaching yourself to create a web application. Grit is working toward that long-term goal.

Illuminator: Suman Mulumudi, Founder, StratoScientific

Anyone who thinks a cell phone's greatest functions are making calls, texting, and taking pictures hasn't met Suman Mulumudi yet. At sixteen years old, he created an app that turns a regular smartphone into a digital stethoscope and heart monitor. The add-on device, called a Steth IO, was created using a 3D printer and everyday materials. As a son of two doctors, Suman has received plenty of encouragement and created a business partnership called StratoScientific with his dad, who is a cardiologist. While awaiting FDA approval for the app, he also created the LesionSizer, which will help doctors treat blocked arteries. For more information about Suman's medical technology visit his company at stethio.com. Read on to learn how Suman is hoping to lower the cost of medical care by creating medical devices with 3D printing.

1. How did you come up with the idea for Steth IO?
Both of my parents are doctors, and as a result I've been exposed to both the patient and the provider side of medicine as I've grown up. In this

process, I noticed that the stethoscope, being as important of a tool as it was, had not changed in almost two hundred years. It had not been brought into the digital age despite the continued difficulty in using it to diagnose heart conditions due to the quiet and low-frequency nature of heart sounds. Starting with this realization, I began looking into some of the techniques that have been used in the past to overcome the current difficulty in interpreting heart sounds. One of the most significant to emerge was visualization using what's called a phonocardiograph. At the time of its invention, it was a rather large machine that was extremely inconvenient to use, so it quickly fell out of favor. With the emergence of the modern smartphone, I found it was a platform that could be the basis of a phonocardiograph. It was as easy to use as the current stethoscope. Having been exposed to 3D printing a number of years back, I began using 3D printing to test out different ways of creating a device that was as easy as a stethoscope but was able to visualize heart sounds in a way that allowed them to be effectively diagnosed. It took many different iterations before I got something that remotely worked.

2. What challenges have you faced in developing a product and setting up a company?

There is no greater challenge than overcoming the human tendency to feel apprehensive toward, if not afraid of, risktaking. Setting up a company and developing a new product are complex tasks and extremely ill-defined. There is no predefined formula on how to go about doing this, although I have quite certainly found many people have very strong opinions on the subject. Coming from high school, in which assignments are given with clearly defined requirements and deadlines, one of the major hurdles I had to overcome was finding a way to effectively make confident decisions while traversing a space without predefined answers and a space that I am completely unfamiliar with. Like so many other challenges in life, the block is entirely mental, and as soon as I was able to internalize the ideology that failing while trying is better than not trying at all, I started to open up to making effective and timely decisions. I still have to remind myself of this quite often. Risktaking is something I imagine I will continue to gain skill in as I gain experience—like all skills, practice makes permanence.

I often struggle with not dwelling on decisions I have already made, especially when those decisions have had adverse effects. I always strive to make the best decisions at every crossroads. Looking back, I am of course now equipped with new information, and it is difficult to accept the fact that at the time, that was the best decision I could have made. It is always important to learn from mistakes, and the only way to do that is to analyze how one makes decisions. It is also important to not let rumination over the past become a distraction. I have made a less-than-ideal decision not because I didn't have the right information, but because I got too bogged down in the previous decisions.

3. What advice would you give teens who are trying to find their passion?
My belief is passion is born out of hard work and grit, not the other way around. I truly believe anyone and everyone can find pleasure in something they produce, and the harder it is to produce, the more pleasure they will draw from its production. Passion is a relentless seeking out of this pleasure. When the going gets tough, that's when it's most important to keep going. I strive to develop a passion for hard work, and I try to do this by placing myself in situations that require greater amounts of grit and tenacity to succeed. As I've found it, whenever I develop a passion for hard work, everything else falls into place. Seek out hard work and situations of grit, and seek them out relentlessly, and through this process, the subject of passion will make itself evident effortlessly and naturally.

4. What activities are you involved with in high school?
My life consists primarily of three spheres: StratoScientific, Lakeside School, and bassoon, which I play as a soloist in my high school orchestra and in the Seattle Youth Symphony Orchestra. I believe that,

in having this broad range of activities in my life, I'm able to create for myself an environment where I not only have a wide range of learning, but I'm also constantly challenged to be flexible in how I learn and pursue success in these various fields.

I think being a bassoonist is probably one of the most rewarding parts of my ongoing education. Musical training demands—more strictly than almost any other field—an absolute attention to detail and sense of discipline. Although discipline is a key for success in all fields, in music it is impossible to achieve even basic success without the discipline to practice effectively and be honest about your own performance. One is required to do this while also creating something beautiful, namely music. For me, musical training has served to show me the importance of discipline, attention to detail, and self-honesty in finding success in any field.

5. What impact has pursuing a dream had on your self-confidence?
I've found self-confidence to be a necessity in pursuing a dream and a set of ideals, and as a consequence, I've had to force it to strengthen. I believe self-confidence is the combination of being able to make decisions, being able to move forward from any decision, and being able to do so in a manner that is in line with discipline and principles. As all of these attributes have improved and changed, my self-confidence has improved as a natural result.

WHAT IF I FIZZLE OUT?

Have you ever been gung-ho about a new activity or project and then suddenly felt burned out? This happens to everyone. It's easy to get caught up in the moment and be excited about something in the beginning. For example, many little kids can't wait to try soccer. They excitedly purchase their cleats and soccer balls, and get a team uniform. They can't wait to get out on the field and play their first game.

How many of those same little kids are signing up for soccer a few years later? Probably not as many.

There's a few reasons people may fizzle out, and it's important to know the difference. Most activities will involve real determination and grit at some point. Many people give up on an activity or lose confidence in their ability when it starts to require hard work. Don't quit something you enjoy just because it needs more effort and a stronger commitment. Give yourself a chance to reboot. Sometimes you just need to recharge your batteries and take a break.

Quitting when it gets tough. *I suck at algebra, so I'll just be happy to pass the class.*

If you feel overwhelmed a lot, then you may need to evaluate the amount of time you spend on the activity and whether you need to scale back. You might discover the activity isn't for you, and if so, then moving on may be the best choice. Or maybe there's something else you'd like to try. Just know why you are quitting and make the decision based on your long-term interest in the activity. It's never best to make decisions in the heat of the moment.

Spotlight
Sana Amanat, Comic Book Editor

If you are a comic book fan, then maybe you have heard of Kamala Khan. She's the first Muslim teen superhero ever featured in a comic. As a Muslim-American, Kamala struggles with figuring out where she fits in. After getting hit with a strange mist, she discovers she has shape-shifting powers, which further adds to her identity issues. This superhero was cocreated by comic book editor Sana Amanat at Marvel Entertainment. Her character (Kamala) mirrors her own life as a teenager. Amanat never felt like she fit in either. She didn't look like her classmates in New Jersey, celebrate the same holidays, or have the same rules and expectations as everyone else. By creating this character, she opened up a discussion about what it means to be a Muslim teen in America, and she gave a whole new group of people a representative in the comic book market. Amanat found a way to use what made her feel different as a teen to help other people. By igniting her spark, she has used her passion for comics to create a positive teen hero.

GET READY, GET SET, GO!

Deciding to try something new is the easy part. It's the execution that gets a bit tricky. Sometimes it's hard to know how to begin. Get off to a great start by approaching new things with the right attitude and with a game plan. For example, if you want to learn tennis, then you may sign up for lessons, find a tennis partner, and schedule time to play. Be determined to give it your best effort. Don't cancel practices, quit when it gets tough, or make excuses. Give yourself credit for learning a sport, trying a new activity, and getting a great workout. You grow with each new experience whether it's a short-term goal or a lifelong passion.

Start by thinking only the best thoughts. Optimists get things done because they believe in themselves and know what they do matters. They know it may take hard work, but they're prepared to apply some grit to accomplish their goals.

Find great mentors. *I'm going to find a photographer to give me pointers on how to take better pictures.*

Compliment yourself along the way. People spend too much time overanalyzing what went wrong instead of appreciating what went right. Keep track of your progress, so you can see how far you've come. The best moments in your life will be when you've worked hard for something, persevered during the tough times, and accomplished your goals. So kick your determination into high gear and don't be afraid to get gritty!

Ignite Your Life Activity

Now that you've learned a little bit about grit, I want you to make a grit list. First, make a list of things you've done that required grit. Did you spend months training for a performance? Have you earned and saved money for something you really wanted to buy? Started a new club at

school? Or created a website from scratch? How did you use grit to achieve your goal? Second, write down a few long-term things you would like to do that will require you to get a little gritty. How can you use some of the skills you've learned in this book to see your long-term goals to the end?

Failing to ask for help or take advice from others. *I don't need anyone's help.*

9

IGNITE YOUR FAILURES

I have missed more than 9,000 shots in my career. I have lost almost 300 games. On 26 occasions I have been entrusted to take the game-winning shot, and I missed. I have failed over and over and over again in my life. And that is why I succeed.
—Michael Jordan, *Greatest Basketball Player of All Time*

ANYWHERE HIGH SCHOOL

The Cosplays are the best teen rock band in town, and Sam is auditioning for them. Since their guitarist, Jules, is moving away, he is a shoo-in to take her place. The band members are his best friends, and he can play along to any song on the radio.

"No offense, but you're not ready for our band," Ryan says after Sam's audition.

"But I thought you needed someone right away, since Jules is moving."

"We do, but you just keep playing the same riffs over and over again. We don't play cover songs, so our guitarist has to know how to produce music."

"Just give me another shot to get it right," Sam says.

"I'll tell you what—the band is taking a break over the summer, so why don't you show us what you've got when we start back up in a few months?" says Ryan. "Don't forget, you have to show me something original."

Sam's first reaction is to be mad at Ryan and the rest of the Cosplays for rejecting him. He decides to pull up some of the band's YouTube videos to see why they think their old guitar player is so great.

She isn't just good; she's awesome. Now Sam understands why Ryan isn't happy with his audition. He needs to learn to create his own music so he can contribute to the band. He is going to take their advice and spend the next few months developing his skills. He starts by making a list of who he can ask to help mentor him and how he can go about achieving his goal of playing with the Cosplays.

DON'T FAIL TO TRY

Sometimes the most amazing stories come out of failures or extreme hardships. People who believe in what they are doing are capable of amazing things. When you love what you do, then every obstacle and challenge is worth it. If you try to be something you're not, then you feel every bump and bruise that comes your way. Some people don't know the definition of *quit* and continue to move forward even when things get difficult. See if you know the answers to the following questions.

* How did the surfers at the Bureh Beach Surf Club in Sierra Leone maintain their passion and optimism for their sport after their country was hit the hardest by the Ebola epidemic?
* How do youth gymnasts spend day after day, hour after hour falling off balance beams and dealing with sore muscles to be one of five girls or boys selected to represent their country in the Olympics?
* How did Manolis Glezos, a ninety-three-year-old man, spend seventy years of his life as a freedom fighter in Greece where he was pepper-sprayed, imprisoned for twelve years, and tortured?

✴ How did a shy singer plagued with anxiety like Adele become a Grammy-winning performer?

The answer to the above questions is resilience. They've all demonstrated it during stressful situations and moments of failure. Although the activities in these four questions have nothing in common, the people behind them share some important character traits. But what does this mean, and how does it apply to you? Let's start by breaking it down.

> Be prepared to handle tough situations. *I'm going to find a tutor to help me in biology since I failed my last test.*

WHAT IS RESILIENCE AND WHERE CAN I GET SOME?

Have you ever seen someone remain calm and cool in a crisis, while someone else falls apart? The ability to cope with tough situations or problems is called resilience. This doesn't erase the stress or worry over life's challenges, but it provides you with the ability to recover or bounce back from them. Remember how we talked about grit in the last chapter? Well, grit and resilience often go hand in hand. Think back to the marathon example. It takes grit to push through the training when it gets difficult to run those miles. If you get injured and can't run the race, then you must rely on resilience to handle the disappointment and bounce back with a positive attitude. Resilience is the difference between being a victim versus being a survivor. If you don't feel like you have resilience right now, don't worry, because you can learn this behavior with a little practice.

Think about how you would handle the following situations: your computer crashes before a school paper is due, an injury before a big soccer tournament keeps you out of a match, your parents are getting a divorce, or your significant other breaks up with you. Would you

Having a complete meltdown when things don't go your way. *I didn't make the school swim team, so I'm never swimming again.*

describe your appearance as calm, cool, and collected? Or do you resemble a two-year-old throwing a tantrum? Most people fall somewhere in the middle with plenty of room for improvement.

While you can't specifically prepare for every upsetting situation that comes your way, you can prepare yourself to handle them better. By building up your resilience, you will be more prepared to handle the tough times. Work on the following key items so you can learn from your setbacks and sail through them with minimum recovery time.

* **Network.** Build relationships with people inside and outside of your family. It's important to have a support system of people you can talk to. Often different people will serve different needs in your life. A trusted coach might be the right person to discuss insecurities you have about your athletic performance, while your best friend is the perfect person to discuss a breakup.
* **Set goals.** Tackling new challenges and having success is a great way to prove to yourself you can handle new situations. Take one step toward your goal every day, even if it is really small. Sometimes the toughest part is getting started!
* **Love thyself.** Be your own best friend. It's hard to make good decisions, bounce back from challenges, or keep your emotions in check if you don't take care of yourself. Give yourself time to relax, have fun, and get a good night's sleep.
* **Problem solve.** Accept that stuff happens. Even if this particular moment stinks, try to come up with solutions to your problem. What can you do to get the best possible outcome?
* **Practice self-control.** Try to take a few deep breaths or count to ten before reacting to an upsetting situation. You don't want to say or

do anything you will regret later, so give yourself a little time to process your emotions.

✳ **Adapt.** Change is inevitable. Life is full of transitions that can be stressful. This never goes away. For example, you may have to deal with moving, changing schools, and making new friends, but think of how the changes affect your parents too. They also have to adapt. Often the changes we are most afraid of turn out to be the best experiences.

Understand that many of life's bad situations are only temporary. *The critique of my online comic book was a total disaster, but I'll blow them away with my next one.*

Spark Quiz
Do You Have Bounce?

New situations come up every day requiring you to make changes. Some of these are good things, and some of them are not so fun. Do you rise up to the challenge, or do you fold up like an accordion? For each situation, choose the answer that best describes how you would react.

1. While walking across the school cafeteria, you trip and almost drop your lunch. You
   a. Laugh it off and keep walking to your seat.
   b. Turn bright red and hurry out of the room.
2. Your best friend moves out of town. You
   a. Keep in touch with your old friend while making new friends at school.
   b. Think school totally sucks now.

3. Your summer job falls through. You
   a. Hustle to find another job.
   b. Accept the fact you're going to be broke.
4. You have three tests and two major papers due next week. You
   a. Prioritize your time and do your best.
   b. Freak out.
5. Your two closest friends can't stand each other. You
   a. Understand not everyone gets along, and spend time individually with them.
   b. Tell them they are both acting like jerks and refuse to talk to either one of them.
6. After a couple of bad games, your coach takes you out of the starting lineup. You
   a. Ask your coach for some pointers and start practicing like crazy.
   b. Pout and feel sorry for yourself.
7. You become the target of some teasing in the school cafeteria. You
   a. Avoid the jerks doing the teasing and chat with your friends.
   b. Pretend to be sick the rest of the week to avoid school.
8. Your dad loses his job and can't help you buy back-to-school clothes this year. You
   a. Offer to babysit, rake leaves, or do whatever it takes to earn some extra money.
   b. Start thinking about how embarrassed you're going to be wearing clothes that are too small from last year.

9. You are nervous about starting a new school. You
   a. Discuss your feelings with your parents and make a plan on how to handle the first day.
   b. Worry about it all night long, get no sleep, and show up for your first day tired.

Did you answer mostly *a* to the above statements? Wow! You are really resilient. You understand that many of life's problems are temporary and won't last forever. Finding solutions and asking for help are part of your troubleshooting plan. Keep up the good work so you'll be able to handle whatever gets thrown your way.

Are your answers mostly *b*? Then now's a great time to work on building your resilience so you don't crash and burn when times get tough. Work on your fear by trying things that scare you in a healthy way, like riding a roller coaster or singing karaoke. Learn to relax by jamming to your favorite music or meditating. Get your good karma flowing by committing a random act of kindness. Get out of your comfort zone by trying new things and creating a tougher and more confident you!

Illuminator: Akash Mehta, Founder, Kids for a Better Future

Kids for a Better Future was founded in 2006 when Akash was just eight years old. Every year this organization run by kids chooses a project to support to help less fortunate kids. They raise money through walk-a-thons, lemonade stands, and fundraising parties. Some of the causes they've supported over the years include a shelter for homeless New York teens, a school for girls in Afghanistan, the rehabilitation of former child soldiers in the Congo, and the Crisis Text Line. They have raised over $100,000 for their programs. Akash and his fellow third graders who started this organization are now ready for college. They've decided to pass down this organization to the next generation of third graders, led by Akash's younger brother, Satya. To find out how you can help kids obtain food, education, and shelter, visit kidsforabetterfuture .org. Read on to learn how Kids for a Better Future use resilience, passion, and dedication to help other people.

1. How did Kids for a Better Future get started?

The first time I thought of this was when I was sitting in the kitchen trying to help my mom wash dishes, but I found that I wasn't good at dishwashing. I sat down and asked my mom what use kids were to the world. She told me we were learning how to be good—we can help the world when we grow up. Plus, when we are kids, we make joy for grown-ups. I said I wanted to do something *now* that makes the world a better place.

2. Do you have mentors and people you look up to?

My mother is the single most inspiring person in my life. She's a lifelong women's rights activist and the founder of the incredible organization Women for Afghan Women. The work she's done and continues to do is really, really tremendous, and I'm so proud of her. She's gone through a lot in her life—she's faced a lot of challenges, but she's managed to really succeed—succeed in securing herself happiness, building a happy family, doing amazing work, and touching the lives of so many people. I have so much to learn from her. I love and respect her so much, and I'm so lucky to have her as a mother.

3. What advice can you give a young person who wants to be a social activist?

It's never too early! Kids are constantly told we need to wait to become adults to help other people—that right now, we should just focus on ourselves. I have two responses to that advice. The first is that all of us, no matter what age, have the ability to make a concrete difference in this world, and therefore we have the moral responsibility to do so. The hundred dollars' worth of food you can raise by running a lemonade stand for a day goes a long way in the life of a kid who doesn't have enough to eat. No matter how old you are, you can make a difference too.

I have another response, as well: you're right. Childhood is a time when we should focus, to an extent, on ourselves—when we should try to learn all we can and try to build ourselves into the adults we wish to be. But we profit immensely by doing work for others. We learn about the world around us. We learn about our power to make a difference. We develop the skills necessary to lead, to inspire, to organize, and to succeed. And if, as adults, we want to be compassionate, determined, and ready to do the work necessary to leave this world in a better place than we found it—well, then there's no better training.

4. What advice can you give teens who are trying to find their passion?
Be bold! There will always be people who tell you to stick to the beaten path and to do what everyone else is doing. They'll tell you that when you're an adult, you can develop your passion—for now, just keep your head down, get through childhood, get good grades, and worry about all that later. Ignore them! Life is about seizing the moment, about following your whims, and about doing what you love. If you don't start now, it'll only be a whole lot harder later.

5. What challenges have you faced while building your organization?
Some of the biggest challenges have been those moments when there's a ton of work to do, I'm pressed for time, and I feel lazy. The solution has always been to reinspire myself into the work I'm doing. I remind myself how important the work I'm doing is to me, and how wonderful its results can be. Once I've re-energized myself, even the dullest work doesn't seem like such drudgery after all.

EPIC FAILS

Believing bad situations last forever. *No one will ask me out ever again.*

An epic fail is a huge, *monumental* disaster! It's regarded as the highest form of failure. Sometimes these are considered failures in the eye of the public (classmates, media, business community, and so on). At other times, these are personal failures where the individual feels the personal humiliation or letdown. Here are some perceived failures when things actually turned out better than just okay.

* **Jennifer Lawrence** tripped on her way up the stairs to collect her best actress award at the 2013 Oscars in front of millions of people. She laughed off the embarrassing moment, made a joke, and became the girl everyone wanted as their new best friend.

* **Kentucky Fried Chicken founder Harland Sanders's** secret chicken recipe was turned down more than a thousand times before being accepted. Now the fast food franchise has over eighteen thousand restaurants all over the world.

* **Winston Churchill** was defeated in multiple political elections. He eventually became prime minister and won the Nobel Prize in Literature.

* **Jerry Seinfeld** was booed off the stage his first time doing stand-up comedy. He became one of the most popular comedians of all time and the star of a major sitcom.

* **Stephen King** received thirty rejections for his book *Carrie*. It went on to sell over 1 million copies in its first year of publication and was made into a feature film and a Broadway show.

* **Melissa McCarthy** was called "tractor-sized" and a "hippo" in a review. She's had the last laugh at her fat-shamers with her huge success as an actress, comedian, and mother.

✳ **Stan Smith** was told he was too clumsy to even be a ball boy at a Davis Cup tennis match. He went on to win eight Davis Cups and even Wimbledon, and he designed a really cool pair of Adidas shoes.

✳ **Anna Wintour** was fired from her junior fashion editor job at *Harper's Bazaar*. She became the infamous editor of *Vogue* and is now the director of all Condé Nast publications.

Learn from your failures. *The next time I try to set up a lawn-mowing business, I'll find a mentor to give me advice.*

✳ **Demi Lovato, Taylor Swift, Christian Bale, Chris Colfer, and Selena Gomez** were all bullied and unpopular at school. They have gone on to become successful celebrities and respected performers.

Illuminator: Sarah Elizabeth Lewis, PhD, Bestselling Author and Art Historian

Sarah Elizabeth Lewis is a multitasking extraordinaire as an art historian at Harvard University, public speaker, and author of *The Rise: Creativity, the Gift of Failure, and the Search for Mastery*. She has served on President Obama's Committee on the Arts and Humanities and was a curator at the Museum of Modern Art and the Tate Modern gallery. She speaks about mastery as something that can be done over and over again versus success, which is usually a celebration of a single moment. The inspirational speech she delivered at the 2014 TED Conference can be watched at ted.com/speakers/sarah_lewis. Read on to see how you can change your view about failure and the creative process.

1. Describe your book The Rise: Creativity, the Gift of Failure, and the Search for Mastery.
The Rise is an atlas of stories about how it is that we truly become our fullest selves, about how incredible, breakthrough ideas actually happen,

from the arts to the sciences, from athletics to entrepreneurial life. I wrote this book not because of the importance I ascribe to failure itself but because of what the irreplaceable advantages from improbable foundations tell us about the nature, needs, and demands of the creative process, about how we each build and fashion our worlds.

2. How are creativity and discovery related to failure?

Most failures are not really failures in the context of innovation, invention, and creativity. As Thomas Edison said after his thousands of aborted attempts to create the lightbulb, "I haven't failed. I have just found 10,000 ways that don't work." The question is, how do we give ourselves enough room to make productive mistakes?

One way is by lowering the feelings of shame and embarrassment that prevent us from even trying things that might go awry. Inventors and artists have long had ways to do this. Playwright August Wilson would start his plays on napkins in restaurants then retreat to his typewriter once the ideas started to flow. His napkin became an incubator, a safe haven, a way of silencing the inner critic. Two Nobel Prize–winning scientists, Andre Geim and Konstantin Novoselov, have an exemplary, playful way of doing this. They have a practice of Friday Night Experiments, times when the lab works on problems outside of the realm of their expertise. Creative solutions and innovative ideas, after all, are often so counterintuitive that they can, at first, look like failure. When we give ourselves permission to be wrong, we find breakthrough ideas that might never have emerged otherwise.

3. There seems to be a lot of pressure regarding academics, athletics, and extracurriculars to view failure as a weakness. How can teens look at it differently?

I'd focus on things that help you become gritty, someone who perseveres in pursuit of your goal despite failure feedback. Grit is a better predictor of achievement, more so than talent or IQ alone. This is what psychologist Angela Duckworth has found. You can develop grit by doing anything—by sticking with a hobby, a side project—from learning to code to learning to kayak.

4. Can you give me a few examples where failure had a positive outcome?
There are too many examples—this is why I wrote *The Rise*, but here are a few: choreographer Paul Taylor's early dance that defined his now award-winning style was a catastrophe—the audience flooded out of the auditorium. Martin Luther King Jr. received Cs not once, but twice in seminary school and went on to lead the nation as the most prodigious orator of his time. The 1930s RKO screen-test response "Can't sing. Can't act. Balding. Can dance a little," was in reference to Fred Astaire. Author J. K. Rowling—who wrote Harry Potter on napkins in restaurants, struggling on welfare as a single mother—said in her Harvard commencement speech that "rock bottom became a solid foundation" on which she built her rise. The title of her talk: "The Fringe Benefits of Failure."

5. If you could go back and give advice to your teen self, what would it be?
Don't worry about being perfect. Focus on growth. Know that your life will be a constant journey and that your greatest gifts and strengths will likely come from your most difficult trials.

Spotlight
Thomas Suarez, Chief Engineer, CarrotCorp

Have you ever played a whack-a-mole app on an iPad or iPod? What about one that involves Justin Bieber? If you have, you were probably playing Thomas Suarez's creation called Bustin Jieber! When Thomas was seven years old, he started computer coding and released his first iPhone application two years later called Earth Fortune. This fortune-teller app would be the first of many for Thomas. By age fifteen, Thomas was developing apps for Apple iOS, Android, Google Glass, and smartwatches through his technology company, CarrotCorp. His next venture is to revolutionize the 3D printing industry with a printer that is ten times faster than the current models. Knowing how much programming has changed his life, he is active with the nonprofit STAR Education to create curricula where youth can learn to code. His TED Talk about kids teaching kids to program has been viewed millions of times. If you would like to bring STAR Education to your school, visit starinc.org. For more information about CarrotCorp apps, go to carrotcorp.com. By igniting his spark, Thomas has proven that you're never too young to become a programmer!

PREPARE TO FAIL

What if you were guaranteed success at whatever you did? Would this change how you decided to spend your time? Would it change what you wanted out of life? How would it affect your hopes and dreams?

Giving up when you fail. *My vlog looks and sounds terrible, so I guess I can't have videos on my website.*

Don't let the fear of failure keep you from taking risks. It's riskier to stand by and do nothing or to do what's safe. And a sure thing is never as rewarding as something you've really worked hard to accomplish. Treat your failures like setbacks that give you an opportunity for growth. With each new failure, you gain insight, new information, and resiliency. You can use this to learn so you can come back stronger and better than ever.

Ignite Your Life Activity

Have you ever failed at something? Maybe it was an epic fail like missing the game-winning shot in a championship game? Or getting up on stage and forgetting all of your lines? Sometimes, simple failures can totally derail us. These can be things like forgetting your homework, tripping in the hall at school, or mispronouncing a classmate's name. It's impossible to be perfect all the time. Everyone has major and minor failures, but how they handle them is what makes them different. If you're going to fail, shouldn't you at least get something out of it? How would you handle the epic and simple failures listed above? Do your answers represent resilience or defeat? Make a list of three different instances when you have failed. Next to each "failure," write down what you've learned from these experiences. Get used to seeing failure as an opportunity for growth!

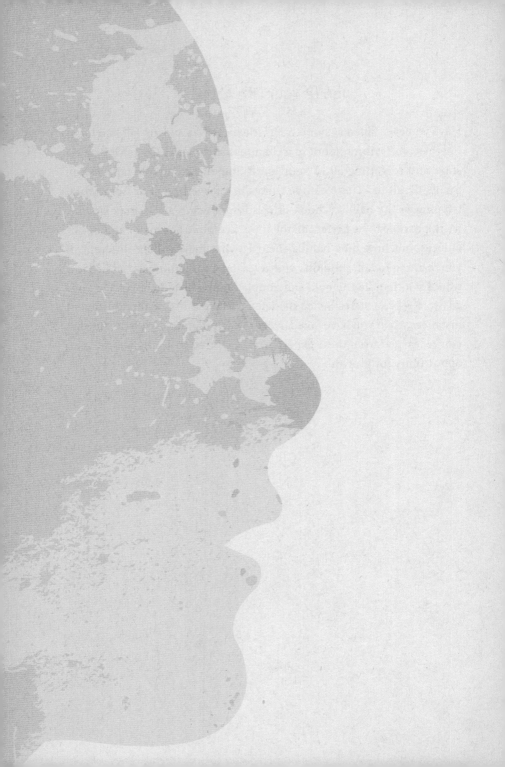

10

IGNITE YOUR WILLPOWER AND CREATE HABITS

The most important thing in life is to stop saying "I wish" and start saying "I will." Consider nothing impossible, then treat possibilities as probabilities.

—*David Copperfield, Magician*

ANYWHERE HIGH SCHOOL

"I'm heading home," Max says to Kirk and Chelsea.

"But we were just getting ready to start another movie," Kirk says.

"I've already spent the entire day at your house," says Max. "I've got some stuff to do with my mom."

"Like what?" Chelsea asks.

"Every Sunday night I help her make dinner. She's teaching me to cook."

"You've got to be kidding me," Kirk says. "Please tell me this is a joke."

"You won't be laughing when we get an apartment and you want to eat," Max says. "I want to know how to make my favorite meals."

"Set an extra plate for me," Chelsea says. "You can cook for me anytime!"

WILLPOWER AND SUCCESS

The easiest way to define *willpower* is "self-control." Every time you resist the urge to do something impulsive, you are demonstrating willpower. You may have plans to study for a big test you have coming up when one of your friends texts to see if you want to go grab dinner. If you are extremely disciplined, then your willpower will kick in and you'll decline the invitation. If you have a hard time saying no to things you want to do versus things you need to do, you may not have a lot of self-control. People with a lot of willpower usually have an easier time handling peer pressure, saving money, avoiding procrastination, and completing homework. They don't let roadblocks and distractions prevent them from completing their tasks.

Exercise willpower when you need it. *I can't go listen to my friend's band tonight because I promised my brother I would help him with his science project.*

Can willpower be taught, or are you just born with it? According to Charles Duhigg, author of *The Power of Habit*, "The best way to strengthen willpower and give students a leg up, studies indicate, is to make it into a habit."[1] A habit is something you do on a regular basis and mostly without thinking. Chances are, your morning routine is a habit. Do you usually shower, get dressed, and brush your teeth in the same way and order every day? If so, it's out of habit.

Habits create efficiency and make your day run more smoothly. Look at a typical routine and how habits work on a daily basis.

6:00 AM Alarm goes off; shower, dress, and pick up room

6:30–7:00 AM Eat breakfast, make lunch, and then go online to read sports headlines

7:30–2:30 PM At school

3:00–4:30 PM Eat a snack and complete homework

4:30–6:00 PM Hang out with friends or chill out at home

6:30–7:00 PM Dinner

7:00–8:30 PM Basketball practice

8:30–10:00 PM Television, video games, or chats with friends

If this person sleeps through his alarm clock in the morning, then the habits are disrupted. His chores don't get done before school, and he doesn't get to go online to read about his favorite teams. After he gets home from school, he still has chores to do on top of homework. He ends up using all of his free time to catch up on the things he missed when he overslept. By the time he goes to bed, he's grumpy and worn out.

Habits are a great way to make permanent improvements in your life and to establish goals. Whether you want to start eating healthier, exercising, writing a blog, or learning a new skill, habits will help you get there. Goals are easier to achieve when they are part of your daily routine. Professional athletes are some of the most habit-based people on the planet. They have established habits for eating, stretching, exercising, and practicing their sport. These habits make it easier for them to stay focused because they don't have to think about what they're going to have for breakfast or what kind of stretches or strength training they'll be doing. They're all automatic because they've made them habits.

Not creating habits. *It's too much work to meditate every day.*

Spark Quiz
How Good Are You at Creating Habits?

When it comes to establishing a new habit, you have to do it every day. Sometimes that means doing it when you'd rather be doing something else. This is when willpower comes in. Your goal may be to plant an organic garden in your backyard, which requires the habit of spending one hour every morning planting, watering, and weeding. Some mornings you may want to sleep in and blow it off. That's when it's time for your willpower to take over. Take this short quiz to see where you are when it comes to creating habits and seeing them through.

1. You're at the mall with your friends and see a T-shirt that's really cool. You've been saving all of your money for spring break, but you really like the shirt. You
   a. Buy the shirt. It's only twenty dollars!
   b. Decide to come back for it when it's on sale.
   c. Save your money. Who needs another shirt?
2. Your best friend is having friends over on Thursday to watch the season finale of your favorite show, but you have a big test the next day. You
   a. Go to your friend's house. You can cram Friday morning.
   b. Study throughout the week when you have time and then go to your friend's house.
   c. Get up an hour early every morning that week to study and go to your friend's house if you feel prepared.
3. You open a new bag of your favorite chips. You
   a. Eat them all. They'll be gone if your sister gets ahold of them.
   b. Eat straight from the bag but make sure you don't eat all of them.
   c. Put a handful in a bowl so you don't eat too many.

4. You've signed up for a weekly fitness class with one of your friends but would rather chill out at home tonight. You
   a. Blow off the class because sometimes you just need a break.
   b. Go to the class but go easy on your workout.
   c. Go to class anyway. Your friend is counting on you.

5. You have a major project due at the end of the quarter. You
   a. Wait until a couple of days before it's due and then pull a couple of all-nighters to get it done.
   b. Finish the project, hand it in, and then find out you left out a few sections.
   c. Read the directions carefully and break it down into sections. You divide the workload by how many days you have to complete the assignment.

6. Your New Year's resolution is to spend more time helping around the house. You
   a. Help out for a few days and then forget about the resolution.
   b. Write your resolution down and post it on your bulletin board so you can get to it when you have time.
   c. Write your resolution down along with specifics like *I will clean my room, do my homework, and load the dishwasher every day without being reminded.*

7. You decide to learn photography because you'd like to improve your Instagram pictures. You
   a. Quit when all of your pictures come out blurry.

b. Find some pointers on the internet and apply them to your picture taking.

c. Take your camera with you everywhere you go and take pictures every day.

If you answered mostly *a*, then you often give in to temptation. Self-discipline is hard when you have to choose between something you want to do and something you should do. A good way to strengthen your willpower is to create a habit and practice it every day for thirty days in a row. After a month, you won't have to think about doing it!

If you answered mostly *b*, then you know how to set habits and know what you need to do to make them stick. Try scheduling a certain time every day when you work on a habit you are trying to create or a long-term project or assignment. Having that time set aside every day will help you when your willpower is tested.

If you answered mostly *c*, then you have a lot of self-control and understand the importance of good habits. Grab some pointers from the interviews in this book on how you can use your willpower and habits to become a great success!

Illuminator: Pooja Dharan, Cofounder, Lil' MDGs

Seventeen-year-old Pooja Dharan is the CEO of Lil' MDGs, a youth empowerment organization focused on the Millennium Development Goals. She cofounded Lil' MDGs with her cousin Dylan Mahalingam when she was six years old and they learned about the goals established by the United Nations to address the most pressing economic and social problems in third-world countries. She serves as the Lil' MDGs spokesperson wherever she is needed, whether it's at a conference or in the media. Her work has been noticed by Archbishop Desmond Tutu, the Dalai Lama, and several United States presidents. After being featured in numerous articles and receiving many awards, Lil' MDGs is well on its way toward achieving its goals. Read on to learn how they are empowering youth all over the world to make a serious impact on the United Nations Millennium Development Goals.

1. What are the Millennium Development Goals?

The Millennium Development Goals (MDGs) are eight goals that were created by the United Nations (UN) in 2000 to address social and economic problems faced by people in third-world countries. These goals include eradicating poverty and hunger, promoting gender equality, reducing child mortality, and much more. These goals were made to be completed in fifteen years, by 2015. However, there are still gaps in what we hoped to achieve by 2015, so the post-2015 development agenda continues the progress toward accomplishing these goals.

2. How did your organization get started?

When I was six years old, I went to India for a visit. At that time, I was much more aware of my surroundings than when I had gone for the first time at two years old. I remember sitting in the cab and seeing homeless people tap on our windows for spare change. I walked on the streets and saw children on the sides begging for food. At the time it upset me to see people living like that, and I wanted to help them out but did not know how.

My cousin Dylan Mahalingam had had similar experiences during his visits before, and when I returned to the United States, the two of us discussed this during one of our conversations. My cousin Ammu, Dylan's sister, told us about the UN MDGs, which focused on a variety of needs for third-world countries, including India. We really liked the idea, and that was the beginning of our organization, Lil' MDGs.

3. What obstacles have you overcome to starting Lil' MDGs?

During the initial stages, we faced a lot of the problems around developing the processes for managing and growing the organization. I was six and Dylan was eight, so we were not old enough to understand the finances and administration required for Lil' MDGs. Our parents supported us a lot in the setup and management activities. We have since overcome these issues and are able to manage a lot of these by ourselves with minimum involvement from our parents.

Lil' MDGs is built on the vision to leverage the power of the internet, digital worlds, and social media to educate, engage, inspire, and empower children in all corners of the world to work together to forward the UN MDGs. During the early years, we encountered issues collaborating with global partners due to language and technical issues. This is also a thing of the past—we have now built and maintain successful relationships with partners on every continent.

4. How has pursuing your passion affected your teen years?

Working at Lil' MDGs has enriched my teen years because it gave me so many different opportunities that opened my eyes to the real world. As a teenager, it can be easy to worry about things such as bad hair days and take a lot of things for granted. In pursuing my passion, I have learned to value what I have because I have realized that a lot of people in many different countries are not as lucky to have the things that most of us take for granted. Lil' MDGs has helped me think of everything in a global context, and helped me develop personally.

5. What advice would you give to teens who are looking for their passion?

My advice for other teens searching for their passion is to keep an open mind. I found my passion through travel, and I love working with children. Lil' MDGs worked well from both those perspectives. However, one does not necessarily need to leave the country to find a cause that they can influence. There are plenty of opportunities all around us, even locally, to assist and empower others.

6. How can people get involved with your organization?
The best way to get involved with our organization is to email us at info@lilmdgs.org and tell us that you want to be a part of our organization! We love hearing from people who are interested in being a part of Lil' MDGs. Also, be sure to tell us why you want to be part of our organization.

TEN TIPS FOR CREATING A HABIT

1. **Know why you are creating the new habit.** To keep your motivation high, you need to know why you are creating the new habit. If your habit is to study more, then you're probably hoping to get better grades. Practicing swimming may lead to a spot on the school swim team. Or exercise will lead to better health, healthier eating habits, and increased strength.

2. **Make it easy.** It's easy to get gung ho over something new and try to accomplish too much at once. This often leads to burnout. For example, if you want to design a website, spend a little bit of time on it every day instead of cramming it into a few all-nighters.

3. **Replace bad habits with a new habit.** If your bad habit is that you snack on junk food all day, then replace that habit with something healthy. Why not start your day with a good breakfast so you're not as hungry later? You can make sure you have healthy snacks available so you aren't

Letting insecurities hold you back. *I don't have what it takes to succeed.*

always reaching for potato chips and cookies to get you through your day. Your mind and body will thank you when you fill up with nutritious food.

4. **Write down your new habit and post it.** Putting a pen to paper and writing down the specifics makes it more official and serves as a reminder to do it. Put it on Post-it Notes and leave them where you can see them. It's difficult to ignore something right in front of your face.

5. **Do it every day.** Practice. Practice. Practice. It's difficult to establish a new habit if you do it only every once in a while. Consistency is key. If you are trying to get into the habit of meditating, then pick a time to meditate every day. If not, it's too easy to fall back into old patterns and not create your new habit.

6. **Don't change it up.** In the beginning, you want to be consistent about how you practice your new habit. The more you keep it the same, the less time you'll spend thinking about it, and the easier it will be to do.

7. **Visualize success.** Starting a new habit isn't always easy, so it can be motivating to picture yourself doing it well, whether it's crossing the finish line, winning a contest, or making new friends. Good habits will have positive outcomes.

8. **Recruit your friends.** There's no reason you have to go it alone. Find a buddy to start the new habit with you, or go online to see if there's a site dedicated to supporting your new habit.

9. **Give it thirty days.** New habits take a while to get established. You may struggle in the beginning and want to quit, but commit to sticking to it for a month. By then it will probably be automatic and part of your daily life.

10. **Reward yourself.** A little self-bribery never hurts, and if it helps you to stick to your thirty-day commitment, then go for it. Your reward may be the thing that keeps you on track on the days you want to give up or quit.

Illuminator: Richard St. John, Author and Public Speaker

Richard St. John can teach you a thing or two about success. He wrote the book *The 8 Traits Successful People Have in Common: 8 to Be Great* based on what he learned from interviewing over a thousand super-successful people like Bill Gates, Richard Branson, and Rupert Murdoch. He delivered a TED Talk on success, which has been viewed over eight million times! On top of being success-ful at talking about success, he's run more than fifty marathons, earned a black belt in judo, and climbed two of the world's highest mountains. You can get to know him better by visiting his website at richardstjohn.com. Read on to learn John's tips for success.

Create habits. *Every morning I review my science notes so I'll be ready for my test.*

1. How do you explain your eight secrets of success to teens?
A teenage girl on a plane once asked me, "What really leads to suc-cess?" So I set out to answer her question and ended up interviewing over a thousand very successful people in many different careers—from accountants, architects, and astronauts to Bill Gates, Richard Branson, Jane Goodall, and the Google founders.

I asked super-successful people in many different careers the same question: "What really helped you succeed?" Their answers were often surprising and the exact opposite of what I believed led to success. For example, I thought all successful people were outgoing and full of self-confidence, but many told me they were shy and full of self-doubt, and it actually helped them succeed. As they destroyed the myths of success, I kept thinking, *I wish someone had told me this when I was a teenager.* And that became the driving force for my research—to give young people the real secrets of success, without any bull. So here they are: the eight traits successful people have in common:

* Passion—Love what you do.
* Work—Work really hard.
* Focus—Focus and concentrate on one thing, not everything.
* Push—Keep pushing yourself.
* Ideas—Come up with good ideas.
* Improve—Keep improving yourself and what you do.
* Serve—Serve others something of value.
* Persist—Hang in there because there's no overnight success.

2. Where does failure fit in?

Failure is something we need to *persist* through, because all successful people fail in one way or another. Of course, nobody wants to fail, but you start failing from the time you're born. When you were a child, you didn't jump up and walk across the floor the first time you tried. You fell down and failed hundreds of times before you could actually walk. But you kept trying, kept learning, kept getting better, and eventually you succeeded at walking. It's the same with anything in life. The incredibly successful people I interview admit they failed many times, and they also attribute it to their success. So when you fail, and you definitely will, think of it as your school *not* your funeral. Just pick yourself up, learn from it, and keep going.

3. How does following your passion lead to success?

The eight traits for success are of equal importance, but I put passion first because if you love what you do, you'll automatically apply the seven other traits that lead to success. If you love it, you'll work hard at it, focus on it, and push yourself. If you love it, you'll think more about it and come up with good ideas. You'll want to improve and get better at it, and serve others what you love. And you're much more likely to hang in and persist when the going gets tough rather than just give up. So passion is the spark that will automatically ignite all the other traits you need in order to succeed.

4. What advice can you give teens who are looking for their passion?

If you haven't found your passion yet, don't panic. You're not alone. When many super-successful people were young, they didn't have a clue what they really loved to do. Even Bill Gates once said, "I was sitting in my room being a philosophical depressed guy, trying to figure out what I was doing with my life."

So how do successful people discover their passion? Well, it doesn't drop into their laps. They have to go out and try a lot of stuff. Like Robert Munsch, who said to me, "I studied to be a priest. That turned out to be a disaster. I tried working on a farm. They didn't like me. I worked on a boat. It sank. I tried a lot of different things that didn't work, but I didn't give up. I kept trying. And then I tried something that did work." Robert discovered he loved writing children's stories, and he went on to sell over 40 million books! Sometimes what you love is right under your nose, disguised as a hobby. Top real estate agent Elli Davis started out as a teacher but didn't like it. What she really loved was reading real estate ads and looking at open houses on weekends. She says, "I was afraid to try real estate, but if I had never tried it, I would never have known how good I could be at it. You must try it. Just do it." Yes, finding a career you love is like finding a person you love. You just have to keep trying, going on a lot of really bad dates, and then one day—bing!—you discover your true passion.

5. If you could go back and give one piece of advice to your teen self, what would it be?

When I was in my teens, I didn't think I'd succeed or go anywhere in life. So if I could go back and give advice to my teen self, here's what I'd say: "Richard, you're shy, insecure, and full of self-doubt. You're not an A student. You don't know what to do with your life, and you often feel like a failure. Well, congratulations! You could be very successful. Because many super-successful people were just like you in their teens—shy, insecure, and not top of the class." So how did they succeed? They kept following the eight traits that really lead to success: passion, work, focus, push, ideas, improve, serve, persist, and as a result they achieved great success. So just like them, if you, too, keep doing the eight traits successful people have in common, you can go as far as you want in life.

Spotlight
Christopher Minafo, Art Student

Have you ever been so focused that you spent over sixty hours on a single project? Christopher did just that when he decided to make a grand send-off to his teen years by painting a large photo-realistic picture of singer Beyoncé. Now he's a student at New York University Steinhardt and has plenty of opportunities to create artwork based on the strong women he admires. He uses digital tools, colored pencils, and paint to create lifelike pictures of artists such as Rihanna, Ariana Grande, and Christina Aguilera. This self-taught artist has managed to capture the personalities of his subjects in his artwork by looking at photographs of them. To watch the video of Christopher creating his Beyoncé painting, visit https://www.youtube.com/watch?v=_wmP_u5KzVs. By igniting his spark, Christopher has created a whole new way for people to appreciate their favorite artists!

CREATE SUPERHUMAN WILLPOWER

Every day you are faced with a million decisions both big and small. Some decisions you make based on what's best for you, and others are made based on what seems easiest in the moment. If you're trying to establish a new habit like getting your homework done early, eating healthier, or practicing an activity every day, then temptation could sabotage your goals.

To create super-strength willpower, prepare for roadblocks. If you know your favorite television show is on Thursday and you're supposed to study for a test, then record the show and watch it after you're done studying. Don't allow bad self-discipline to interfere with a habit you're trying to establish. Watching your favorite show will be a great reward when you can kick back and relax because all of your work is done.

The more habits you create, the stronger your willpower will be. Habits put you into autopilot because they become second nature. You don't have to think about doing them because they are a part of your routine. With super habits, your days will go much smoother and you'll be amazed at how much you get accomplished. Once you get started you won't have to worry about a lack of self-control getting in the way!

Giving in to temptations. *I'm going to skip baseball practice to go to the beach with my friends.*

Love what you do. I love volunteering at the animal shelter to help dogs and cats get adopted.

Ignite Your Life Activity

Are you ready to create a new habit? Grab your calendar and let's get started. Pick a habit that's interesting to you—don't pick one for your parents, your teachers, or your friends. Now that you've chosen a habit, write it down. This is something you will practice every day for thirty days. For example, if you wanted to get stronger, then you might decide you want to do thirty push-ups, sit-ups, and jumping jacks every morning as soon as you wake up. Figure out a reward for yourself when you make it to the end of the thirty days, and write it down next to your habit. Visualize yourself succeeding in your new habit. You're only thirty days away from reaching your goal!

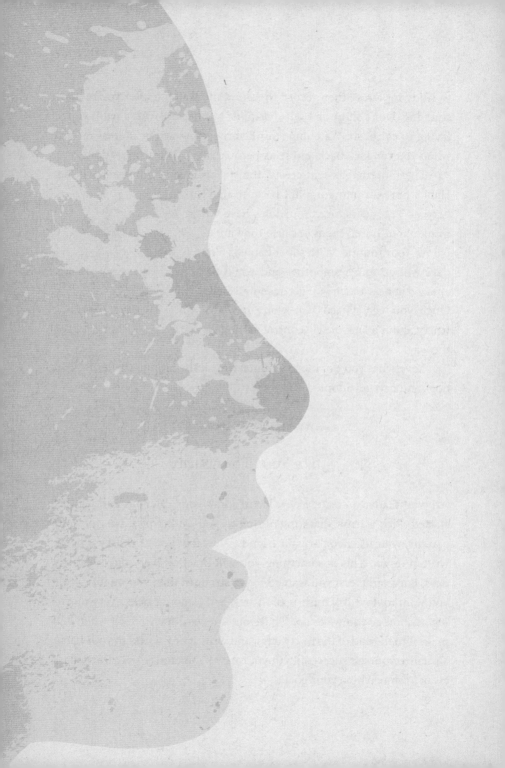

11

IGNITE YOUR FUTURE NOW!

You have to stay true to yourself. And don't be afraid—
even though people might say that what you're doing
isn't cool or isn't right—I promise you, you will not regret it
if you stay true to who you are and what you do.
Because there is no other reason I'm up here today.
—*Emma Stone, Actress*

ANYWHERE HIGH SCHOOL

"Hey, Cameron, your sister told me you aren't planning on going to college next year. Is that true?" Katherine asks.

"Yeah. College isn't my thing," Cameron says. "I need a break from school."

"So have you got a job lined up or something?"

"Nah. I don't want to work for somebody else. I'll probably start my own thing."

"Do you have any idea what that is?" says Katherine.

"Not really. I haven't really given it much thought."

"Well, you better figure it out, because I don't think your parents are going to be too happy going to work every day while you lie around on their couch."

Cameron knows Katherine is right. He needs a plan for next year. His mom is pretty good about talking things through with him, so maybe after dinner he'll ask her for some advice.

START WORKING ON THOSE FUTURE GOALS

Are you ready to get started? You may think you're supposed to sit around and wait until after high school or college graduation to get started on your future, but that's not true. Whether you're ten, sixteen, or eighty-five years old, you can start anytime. You can do research, learn new skills, and start planning for a brighter future. So why wait around? There's no better feeling than setting goals and then achieving them. Your future is now! It helps to know what a goal really is and how to set one.

In 1968 professor and psychologist Dr. Edwin Locke and Dr. Gary Latham developed a goal-setting theory that continues to be used today.[1] It's built around the idea that a goal should be challenging and very specific in order to have the best chance of success, and it's a great tool for igniting your spark. Based on their theory, there are five igniters:

* **Be clear.** Write out your goal with lots of details. Decide how you will measure your success and how often. Most important, make sure your goal excites you!
* **Present a challenge.** Is your goal hard but not overwhelming? How can you reward yourself along the way to keep your motivation high?
* **Make a commitment.** Visualize how awesome it will be when you achieve your goal.
* **How am I doing?** Whether you're analyzing yourself or asking other people to give you feedback, it's important to check your progress on a regular basis. You may need to make some changes to keep things on track.

✳ **How hard is this going to be?** Don't let your goals stress you out! If they seem too hard, then consider breaking them down into smaller goals.

Finishing projects only when you are pushed. *I'll work on my graphic design idea if my dad reminds me.*

Here's an example of how this works:

Goal: I want to run a 5K (3.1 miles) by the end of the summer. I will follow Cool Running's Couch to 5K program for nine weeks and track my progress on their free computer application. Every week that I correctly follow the program, I will plan a special outing with one of my friends. By keeping track of my workouts, I can make sure I'm increasing my distance every week. At the end of the summer, I will sign up for a race and achieve my goal by crossing the finishing line.

Be specific with your goals. *I will practice yoga three times a week for one hour for the next thirty days.*

Spark Quiz
Are You Self-Motivated?

Most of us are pretty good at setting goals. We set them all the time. We say things like, "Next semester I'll make the honor roll," "By the end of the summer, I'll be able to run three miles," or "I'm going to save enough money to buy a video game." This is usually where we stop when it comes to making goals. We make statements and then move on with our lives and forget them. How many of these goals do we actually reach? Not very many. For a goal to have a fighting chance, you have to be self-motivated. To see if you've got what it takes, answer *true* or *false* for each statement.

1. I know I can achieve the goals I set for myself.
   True or False
2. I can visualize myself achieving my goals.
   True or False
3. I always try my hardest to reach my goals.
   True or False
4. I don't obsess about failing.
   True or False
5. I reward myself for achieving my goals.
   True or False
6. I set goals that are realistic.
   True or False
7. I work on my goals without being told by other people.
   True or False
8. I plan out how I will achieve my goals.
   True or False
9. I ask for help when I run into a roadblock.
   True or False
10. After I hit my goal, I start planning for my next set of goals.
    True or False

For every time you answered *true*, pat yourself on the back. Your spark is ignited, and you are ready to kick some serious butt! You aren't messing around when there's something you want to achieve. You do what it takes to get the job done.

If you answered *false* for several statements, then improve your odds by asking yourself the following questions when you set a goal: Is it achievable? Is the goal important to me? Have I given myself enough time to work on my goal? Do I have the right attitude?

Illuminator: Eliza McNitt, Film Writer and Director

Eliza McNitt is in her early twenties and has already received over fifty film festival nominations and awards. In 2009, while in high school, she won first place in the Intel International Science and Engineering Fair for her research on honeybee colonies. *O, The Oprah Magazine* called her a "teen genius," and she went on to make a film about her science research called *Requiem for the Honeybee*. This marked the beginning of her filmmaking career, and she has created one award-winning film after another ever since. She is a recent graduate of NYU's Tisch School of the Arts, specializing in film and television, and has started her own production company. Her short film credits include *The Magic Motorway*, *Violet*, *The Ninth Train*, *My Ketchup Smiles*, *The Fragment*, and *Without Fire*. Her documentaries include *Smashing Science*, *Requiem for the Honeybee*, and *Kougie & Me*. Her most recent project is a short film, *Artemis Falls*, which follows an astronaut as she orbits into space. To see her movie trailers, visit elizamcnitt.com. Read on to learn how an interest in honeybees led her to a career in filmmaking.

1. How did your high school science project about honeybees come about?

The turning point in my relationship with honeybees came during a visit with my grandfather who, while a chemical engineer at MIT, taught Army officers how to defend against nerve-gas attacks during WWII.

Unnerving is a good way to describe what he told me about the carcino-genic properties of the insecticides that were likely to have been used on an apple I was about to eat. It wasn't too late to wash the apple. But while pouring honey in my tea, I had an ominous thought. Don't bees make honey from the nectar of apple blossoms? And aren't those blossoms also sprayed with insecticides? These questions led me down a two-year path of science research, investigating the role of the pesticide imida-cloprid and its role in colony collapse disorder—the disappearance of honeybees around the world.

2. Did that experience impact your decision to go into film production?
Science led me to filmmaking. During a lecture in AP English, a fel-low classmate whispered to me, "C-SPAN is holding a documentary filmmaking contest to inform Obama about the nation's most pressing issue."

"Colony collapse disorder!" I blurted out, nearly falling off my chair and interrupting Mrs. Johnsmeyer's lecture.

I'd won first place at the Intel science fair for my research on honeybees, but the audience I was able to reach out to was limited to scientists and environmentalists—I thought this documentary compe-tition would be an opportunity for me to transform my research into a film. I traveled to Florida and Pennsylvania to interview leading scien-tists and beekeepers.

I was in a bee suit holding my little HD camera in a swarm of bees when I realized I was fascinated by this. Not the sweaty suit, but the process of making a movie. There was a real adventure involved in the creation of a film. Our documentary *Requiem for the Honeybee* won first place in C-SPAN's competition and was broadcast internationally.

As a competitor in science fairs, I told a narrative about my research—my hypothesis, the materials I used, how I came across my conclusion—and I realized what interested me all along was the process of storytelling.

3. Where do you think all of your determination came from to pursue your passion at such a young age?

I was never as fast as our star players on the lacrosse team. I think a lot of my determination has come from not being the best player on my sports team or the first-place winner in every competition. My parents have always supported me and created an environment where making mistakes is an opportunity to develop. I think that's the most important thing to do, fail gracefully.

4. What advice can you give a young person who wants to be a writer or filmmaker?

Make films. Make mistakes. Be vulnerable. One of the best pieces of advice I've received from directors like Alexander Payne is to just keep at it. If you want to be a filmmaker, get a camera and a couple of friends and go make a movie. And it probably will not be great, so make another one. And another one. Filmmaking is about collaboration and communication with your peers. And it's important to make mistakes in order to find your voice. We live in this digital age where you can just pick up a camera and shoot, so there is no excuse anymore. I need to keep telling myself that.

5. What are some of the biggest challenges young people face in discovering who they are?

I'm still trying to discover who I am. In high school I always felt this pressure to fit in. But I never did. And I think that's really important. I did theater, was student body president, and was competing in science fairs. I went from a Montessori school with five people in my grade to a high school of three thousand. That transition helped me realize I didn't fit in with the crowd and eventually I just needed to embrace that side of me. As a filmmaker, the most powerful stories are ones you have a strong personal connection to. And I think that's a big part of figuring out who you are. I still have a long way to go before I even figure out about myself fully. But I think uncertainty is an important part of this journey.

6. *Where do you see yourself in ten years?*

I want to change the way people see film. Like every independent filmmaker, I dream of having a film at a festival like Sundance, SXSW, or Tribeca. But in ten years from now, the landscape of film will shift dramatically. I imagine a future where scientists and storytellers collaborate to create immersive, story-based work. In ten years from now, I hope to direct my first feature film and be filming my second. The best opportunities right now are in television. I'd like to be the show runner of a television show and bring science to the forefront of entertainment. At the very least, in ten years, I hope to not have to live with roommates.

HOW A NEW SKILL IS DEVELOPED

You learn how to do new things all the time whether it's intentional or accidental. It might be making an omelet, doodling in bubble letters, or assembling a piece of furniture. These are all new experiences you are adding to your skill set. Small tasks will help you learn more complicated ones in the future. For example, cooking an omelet may prepare you for making a more difficult recipe down the road since you're now familiar with cooking measurements, reading a recipe, and how to operate kitchen appliances. Developing a skill often goes through three main stages:

1. **You are introduced to a new activity.** Your dad takes you out driving for the first time.
2. **You are showing improvement in the activity and are making fewer mistakes.** You can drive the car without gripping the wheel, hopping up on curbs, or making your father nervous.

3. **The skill becomes more automatic and you don't experience much of a change in your performance.** You are confident behind the wheel of a car. Many things like using your turn signal or looking in your rearview mirror are now automatic.

TURNING YOUR SKILL INTO A TALENT

Are you ready to take your skills to the next level? Then try what pros like LeBron James and Serena Williams do when they want to improve their game. They focus on the quality, not the quantity, of their practice. When you learned to tie your shoes, did you just play with your shoelaces? Of course not! You practiced how to do it step by step until you got it right. That's quality time.

Practicing without purpose. *I want to get better at swimming, but practicing the same stroke over and over again is so boring.*

Deliberate practice is when you practice a very specific activity in order to improve your performance. Each activity is broken down into the smallest segments so you can master each individual step. It's important to have a way to measure your progress and to know if you are doing each step correctly. Then it's time to practice, practice, practice.

For example, if you wanted to improve your tennis serve, you would first need to break it down into parts—body position, ball toss, grip, back swing, reach, overhead swing, and the finish. Then you would pick just one of these elements to work on at a time and track your improvements. For ball toss, you could figure out how high you want to toss it, the angle, and where you want it to land. You might set your goal at a hundred tosses a day and keep a tally of how many tosses land in the right place. Tossing a ball up in the air a hundred times may not sound like a lot of fun, but deliberate practice is meant to get you results.

What if you're not an athlete? How can you incorporate deliberate practice into your life? Musicians, dancers, and artists have been doing this for years. Even someone who wants to get better at playing the video game Minecraft could use it to focus on strategy instead of mindless gaming. Every activity involves skills, from sports, art, or public speaking to making friends or planning a party. They all have steps that can be broken down and perfected. Doing this will take your performance from good to great!

> Use deliberate practice to increase performance. *I'm going to break my piano piece down into small sections and work on one at a time until I get it right.*

Illuminator: James Anderson, Founder of Thinkspace and Developer of Zest

James Anderson is the seventeen-year-old founder of Thinkspace, a student-led space in schools where students can learn coding to create applications and websites. The spaces are cool, high-tech, and a great place to hang out. Over four hundred schools have expressed an interest in creating their own Thinkspace. James has been featured in various publications like *Wired*, CNET, and ZDNet. His latest ventures include speaking at TEDxTeen Conferences and creating a new digital retail experience with his Zest application. To find out more about his food and beverage ordering app visit http://zesthq.co. Read on to learn how he took his passion of coding to the next level.

1. Where did the idea for Thinkspace come from?

I was always frustrated by the dull and uninspiring computing rooms in my school, which hindered creativity and productivity instead of promoting it. Ever since the age of seven I have been coding and building various projects of my own, so I wanted to bring the opportunities I had to other people. Teachers didn't know how to properly code themselves, and the resources weren't there to build real-life products that could potentially be in the hands of millions.

I had been fortunate enough to visit the headquarters of large tech companies like Google and Facebook—their office environments are fun, welcoming, and spacious. I began to wonder what it might look and feel like to have these beautiful environments inside schools. That's when Thinkspace was born—a space in schools around the world where students can come and learn how to code, modeled to look and feel just like the funky offices inside some of these large tech company head-quarters. It's incredibly fascinating how if you change the environment students are working in, it can drastically change their mind-sets. When I founded Thinkspace with my partners Ollie Bredemeyer and Kamram Malik, I was amazed to see people from all walks of life coming in and enjoying turning their dreams into digital products that could be shared with their peers—but more importantly, with the rest of the world. Some of these people would have previously slated those who coded, calling it "uncool" or "a waste of time." Because we changed the environment that these activities took place in, it completely changed the way they think about coding. That was certainly one of the most rewarding parts about founding Thinkspace, and I think it can be applied to so many other areas of school and education as a whole.

2. What advice would you give to teens who are trying to find their passion?

My best advice to young people with a passion, talent, or idea, want-ing to take it to the next level, is to do what you can with what you have. You have to start small and build from there. That's what I did with Thinkspace—initially it was just a space inside our own school, then we realized that we could turn this project into an organization and expand to the rest of the world. We never set out with the intention of building an organization or making money (which we don't anyway, since Thinkspace is a nonprofit)—we simply wanted to make coding fun, accessible, and free for everybody. Remember that virtually everybody in this world who has ever been successful was once a beginner and started from nothing, with nothing.

3. What obstacles did you run into when you were first starting out?

It was very difficult balancing education and starting a business at the same time. Before long, I realized that I couldn't successfully juggle both—I had to sacrifice one; otherwise everything would be at risk of failing. I chose to drop out of high school in 2014, a year before everybody else would finish. This was scary and difficult but also one of the best decisions I have ever made. Since dropping out of school with little qualifications I have been much more vulnerable, which I think is mostly a really good thing because it gives you some perspective on life and allows time to plan where you want to go. The places I have traveled and the people I have met in my time outside of school have been hugely inspiring to me and have given a unique insight into life that I otherwise wouldn't have had.

4. What have been the most important things that have led to your success?

We have been incredibly fortunate to be surrounded by a small army of people who have believed in us from the start. A friend of mine, Richard Knox-Johnston, started iwantoneofthose.com in 2000 and then later sold it for over $14 million. He has since dedicated the rest of his life to helping young entrepreneurs turn their ideas into reality, and for that I have the utmost respect for him. Richard has been by our side through the extreme highs and extreme lows of the start-up life which has been invaluable to our success thus far. Others like Richard Branson, Stephen Fry, and Dick Costolo have supported me on my personal journey and helped spread the word through the immense power that is social media. This was one of the greatest challenges: how do we get an idea that started out in one school to spread around the world? Through the insane amount of press coverage we received and the generous support from our backers, we managed to reach over 15 million people on the launch of Thinkspace, resulting with over four hundred emails from schools interested in building their own.

5. What are you working on at the moment?

Most recently, I cofounded Zest with my sixteen-year-old business partner George Streten—using our mobile app, you can order and pay for food and beverages from carefully curated independent cafés and restaurants before you arrive, at the tap of a button. Zest currently operates across Central London. We have partner stores in seven of thirty-two London boroughs, and our goal for the end of 2016 is to launch in all thirty-two boroughs. We've received an investment from one of the UK's biggest retailers, John Lewis, and support from Stephen Fry, Finn Harries, Joanna Shields, and others.

INTERNSHIPS AND LOOK-SEES

Do you want to know what a real workday is like for a particular career? Then find an internship where you can get experience working in the field. You will gain valuable work skills and get an inside look at the pros and cons of that job. Through this on-the-job training, you will get exposure you wouldn't gain in the classroom. Take the opportunity to get to know your coworkers and learn about their jobs as well. You may find a mentor who can help guide you as you start making future plans.

Making your goals too hard. *I will learn to code a video game by next month.*

If you can't find an internship or can't commit the time, then set up a look-see. This is when you shadow a person for a day so you can see a job in action. Most people are flattered to have someone interested in their career field and will be more than happy to answer your questions. You can contact the company directly to inquire about shadowing someone, or talk to your school guidance counselor about help setting up a look-see. Either way, you won't believe how many people are eager to help you when you take the initiative.

Spotlight
Rachel G. Fox, Day Trader, Fox on Stocks

Do you know the difference between technical and fundamental analysis when it comes to looking at company stocks? Seventeen-year-old Rachel Fox can tell you! This actress, indie rocker, and college student is also the voice behind the *Fox on Stocks* blog. Her stock trading philosophy focuses on the effect pop culture events or people have on company stock prices. For example, the success of *The Hunger Games* franchise could lead her to researching the stock share prices of movie studio stocks and merchandise manufacturers. So far, her research has paid off. She consistently has double-digit profits, and she hopes other teens will follow in her footsteps by opening their own stock trading accounts. Her blog is a wealth of information for people who are interested in learning more about the stock market. She has created videos to start people down the path of learning the core concepts behind money investment. To learn more about how she outperforms the market, visit foxonstocks.com. By igniting her spark, Rachel has inspired a whole new generation of people to take an active interest in the stock market!

WHERE ARE YOU GOING?

It's never too early to start asking yourself where you're going. You can start by developing your after–high school plans. Are you going to college? Getting a job? Or starting a business? A lot of options open up for you when you become an adult. Be prepared to take advantage of the possibilities.

If you have fun doing what you do, then you will be more productive. You will spend more time thinking about it, learning about it, and doing it. Focus your goals around those things that bring you enjoyment. The most important things that happen to you will be the result of effort, so invest your time wisely. Gaining new skills and improving your performance are great motivators. Use deliberate practice to get yourself to the next level, and set yourself up for a bright future.

Constantly work on new skills. *I'm going to have my dad show me how to change a flat tire on a car.*

Ignite Your Life Activity

Deliberate practice is an excellent way to increase performance and be rewarded for your effort. If you've ever seen the show *The Voice*, then you've seen deliberate practice in action. During their coaching sessions, the competitors are often asked to practice the same note over and over again until they can hit it just right on a consistent basis. You can try this at home with your own goals. Deliberate practice works with anything where performance can be improved. Write down something you would like to improve, and then break that activity into steps. For one week just practice that one step. By the end of the week, you can decide if you're ready to move to the next step. You don't need to have a coach like Adam Levine or Blake Shelton to ignite your spark. You can be your own talent scout!

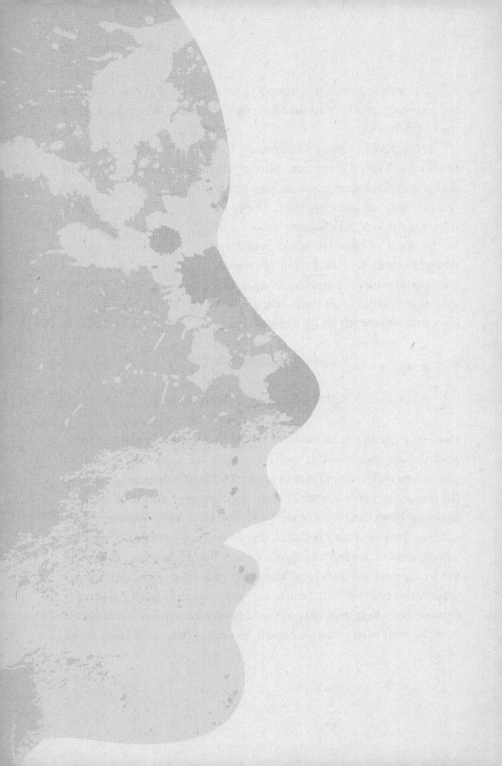

12

YOU'VE GOT THIS

You have to be unique, and different, and shine in your own way.
—Lady Gaga, Performer

GET IGNITED!

So you've made it this far in the book and have a few ideas of some things you want to try. Make a list. Don't spread yourself too thin by trying everything at once. The key to going for it is to want it really, really badly—not kind of want it, maybe want it, or sort of want it. Half-baked effort is a waste of time. Put a star next to every item on your list meeting the qualification for "wanting it really, really badly." For example, maybe the information you read in chapter 6 about volunteer work sparked some interest. If so, you can start with the resource list at the end of the book to see if you can find a good match.

The key is to get started. Anyone can read a book or hear a lecture and get inspired. It's easy to get pumped up with a new idea and then fizzle out when it's time to execute. Your mission is to pick a few things you've learned in this book that interest you and to put them into practice. You will never regret pursuing your interests. This is about *you* helping *you* move closer to your dreams. So get moving!

Spark Quiz
What Have You Learned?

Are you ready to jump out of bed in the morning with a purpose? Here's the big test to see if you've learned anything about yourself by reading this book. At this point I hope you're pumped up and ready to try some new things. We've discussed how habits, grit, and great relationships can help you along the way. You may get a few bumps and bruises, but some of your greatest rewards in life will come from struggle, hard work, and focus. Let's see if you're ready to get started on your journey. Answer *true* or *false* for the following statements.

1. I have dreams I want to pursue now and in the future.
   True or False
2. I know how to set and achieve my goals.
   True or False
3. I can stick with something even when it gets tough.
   True or False
4. I know that most setbacks and challenges are temporary.
   True or False
5. I appreciate my talents and don't beat myself up over my shortcomings.
   True or False
6. Failing is not a reason to give up.
   True or False

7. I understand people on social media showcase only what they want you to see.
   True or False
8. I know how to balance school, friends, family, and activities.
   True or False
9. I'm loyal and trustworthy to my friends.
   True or False
10. I think I'm a pretty cool person just the way I am.
    True or False

Congratulations for every time you were able to answer *true*. You have officially ignited your spark in those categories! Half the fun is in the journey, so enjoy the ride while getting to know yourself. For every *false* answer, go back to the chapter that covers the information to refresh your memory. Your job is to do whatever it takes to turn your *false* answer into a *true*. Gather more information on the internet, enlist the help of your friends and family, and do some soul-searching. You'll be one step closer to taking charge of your life.

GET OFF THE FENCE!

If your favorite statements are "I don't know how" or "I could never do that," it's time to remove them from your vocabulary. Make a decision and see it through to the end. Quit sweating it once the decision is made, and use your grit to overcome any challenges.

Put together an action plan. Would you get in your car and start driving to another state without mapping out your route first? Or start answering a homework problem before you've read the question? Of course not! It would be a total disaster. Do your research. Don't let vague details and lack of information give you the wiggle room to bail on your goal. You'll be so happy if you just go for it and accomplish your mission.

This is your chance to evolve. Just like you transitioned from being a kid to a teen, this is your opportunity to start developing what kind of adult you will be. You can change your path in life if you want to badly enough, or explore new activities, or develop new relationships, or add meaning to your schoolwork, or do anything that makes you super excited instead of counting down the days until you are officially an adult. Whatever you want to improve, you can do it right now. You just have to take that first step to get yourself moving.

DOING IT THE SPARK WAY

* Embrace your uniqueness. Your differences make you a special, interesting, and one-of-a-kind person.
* Base your self-confidence on your inner beauty. Don't let your outer beauty define you. You are more than your looks!
* Be authentic with your friends. Let them get to know the real you instead of the person you think they want to see.
* Make school projects and assignments meaningful. They are a great opportunity for you to research and explore your interests.
* Open yourself up for new activities and opportunities. Hobbies are a fun way to relax, develop new skills, and meet people who like to do the same things.
* Believe your dreams can come true. If you want something badly enough, then go for it and make it happen.
* Get gritty. Don't quit when things get tough. Work through problems and you'll be rewarded by achieving your goals.
* Set yourself up for success by setting goals. Write them down and add the steps you need to take in order to achieve them.

✳ Practice with a purpose. With deliberate practice, you will increase your performance in any activity.

✳ Bounce back from failure stronger than ever. Use what you learn from your setbacks as an opportunity for growth.

✳ Create habits so your days go off without a hitch. They keep you on pace and make it harder for temptations to creep in.

✳ Have fun! This is your life, so live every day to the fullest.

YOU'VE GOT THIS

If you're reading this sentence right now, then you've probably read this entire book (unless you're one of those people who skips ahead to the end). That's great! You've already taken the first step toward igniting your spark. Keep that momentum going by integrating some of the things you learned about yourself through the quizzes and writing activities into your daily life. You can start with small changes or go big—this is your journey.

It's never too late or too early to take action. You are a work in progress and will be under construction for the rest of your life. Part of what makes you interesting, amazing, and unique is that you're always changing. You can design any type of life you want for yourself, and if you don't like it, you can change it.

You may be wondering, *Where does my spark come from? How will I know if it's been ignited?* It might be ignited quickly and clearly like love at first sight, or it might take time to develop with your interest getting brighter and brighter. If you are lucky, it will strike you like a lightning bolt. You'll try some new activity and just know you've found your perfect match. But for most people, you won't find your niche right away. You'll have to expose yourself to many new things and people to find what's right for you. And when you find that activity, that friendship, that dream that ignites your spark, you'll feel the connection. Doors will open and you'll find meaning in what you do.

But most important of all, igniting your spark is fun! It's an amazing feeling when you have passion for what you do. Once the momentum starts and you are taking your life in the direction that makes you happiest, everything else starts to fall into place. It's a domino effect. When your personal identity shines through, you are attracted to activities that support your dreams, and to like-minded people, and to positive relationships. So get out there and ignite your spark and love who you are on the inside and out!

ACKNOWLEDGMENTS

Writing a book can often be a very solitary experience, but in my case I had twenty-two amazing interviews to keep me company along the way. A special thanks to all of those people who took the time to answer my questions and who inspire the rest of us to dream a little bigger. I can't wait to see what you do next.

I want to thank the team who helped to create this book. My in-house editing team of Lindsay Brown and Emmalisa Sparrow—you make everything you touch so much better. To the rest of the team, Sara Blum, Devon Smith, Bill Brunson, Whitney Diffenderfer, Ruth Hook, Jackie Hooper, Ali Shaw, and Ashley Van Winkle—your contributions to this book were invaluable.

I would like to thank my grandmother, Joan Baker, who is always cheering me on from Belleville, Kansas. And to Bruce Freshwater for planting the seed for me to write a book even before I knew I was a writer—you are missed every day! To my neighbors and friends who treat me like family—your graciousness is more inspiring than any book I could ever write. To my in-laws, Gary and Jeanette, and my brother-in-law, Nick, you are the definition of kindness.

A special thanks to my mother, Cheri Freshwater, who's always willing to jump on a plane to take the boys to ball practice, fold laundry, and make sure we are fed. To Max and Jack who are my biggest source of inspiration and the reason I wrote this book. And the biggest thank-you to my husband, Scot, for always encouraging me to focus on my dreams. Every year I feel more blessed to be standing by your side.

NOTES

Chapter 1

1. Alexandra Robbins, *The Geeks Shall Inherit The Earth: Popularity, Quirk Theory, and Why Outsiders Thrive after High School* (New York: Hyperion, 2011), 7.

Chapter 2

1. Liz Braun, "Justin Bieber: 2014's Most Annoying Celebrity," *Ottowa Sun*, December 30, 2014, http://www.ottawasun.com/2014/12/29/justin-bieber-2014s -most-annoying-celebrity.

Chapter 4

1. Shaun Verma, "Mission of #MDJunior," MDJR.org, accessed February 3, 2016, http://mdjunior.org/mission.php.

Chapter 8

1. Angela Lee Duckworth, "Grit: The Power of Passion and Perserverance," TED video, 6:12, April 2013, http://www.ted.com/talks/angela_lee_duckworth_the _key_to_success_grit.

Chapter 10

1. Charles Duhigg, *The Power of Habit: Why We Do What We Do in Business and Life* (New York: Random House, 2014), Kindle edition eBook, chapter 5.

Chapter 11

1. "Locke's Goal-Setting Theory," MindTools, accessed July 17, 2017, http://www .mindtools.com/pages/article/newHTE_87.htm.

RESOURCES

In this section you'll find all kinds of resources to help you ignite your spark, figure out who you want to be, and help get you through some of the dark times. Take a look through the list and see what sparks your interest and what speaks to you most. You never know where you might find your next big dream!

SPARK UP YOUR EXPERIENCE

Giving-Back Resources

American Red Cross. This national organization provides medical and relief aid to people all over the world. http://redcrossyouth.org/.

Do Something. Join millions of teens who are making a positive impact on the world by starting and becoming involved in social campaigns. http://www.dosomething.org/.

Generator School Network. Do you need help planning your project, or want to find other people interested in your cause? This site provides project-planning tools to get you started. https://gsn.nylc.org/plan/.

Habitat for Humanity. Help build a house for a family in need. http://www.habitat.org/youthprograms/.

Kids Are Heroes. This nonprofit is an incubator for young social entre-preneurs, whether you need an idea on how you can effect positive change in the world or want to showcase what you are doing. http://www.kidsareheroes.org/.

Kids for a Better Future. Find out how you can join this movement run by kids to provide food, shelter, and education to kids from less fortu-nate circumstances. http://www.kidsforabetterfuture.org/.

LemonAID Warriors. Learn how to turn your party into a Philanthro-Party so you can raise money for your favorite cause. http://www.lemonaidwarriors.com/.

Scenarios USA. Do you have something to say about a social issue? Put your writing and film skills to good use by telling your story. https://scenariosusa.org/.

Youth Volunteer Corps. Make friends and help your community by performing team-based services. http://www.yvc.org/.

Inspirational Resources

Daily Good. To read uplifting and inspirational daily stories, bookmark this site. http://www.dailygood.org/.

Foundation for a Better Life. Visit this website often to read positive messages, view public service campaigns, and learn about local heroes. The foundation has worked with some of the most popular musical recording artists of all time to bring their uplifting messages to life. http://www.values.com/.

Motivation. Do you need some extra motivation for your next project? Then log in to this site for your daily dose of inspirational ideas. http://www.motivation.com/.

Operation Beautiful. Help end negative self-talk by leaving positive messages in public places. http://www.operationbeautiful.com/.

The Dream Share Project. Follow Chip Hiden and Alexis Irvin around the country as they interview people who have found their passion in life. http://www.thedreamshareproject.com/.

Just-for-Fun Resources

Artist's Network. Are you an artist in the making? Do you love to be creative and learn new ways to express yourself? This site will help you learn new techniques and possibly inspire your next great project. http://www.artistsnetwork.com/.

Craftster. Over 1 million readers per month become a part of this online community to show off their DIY projects and get ideas for their next project. http://www.craftster.org/.

Duckworth Lab. How much grit do you have? Take this short quiz by the University of Pennsylvania to find out. https://sites.sas.upenn.edu /duckworth.

The Great Kindness Challenge. Gather a group of friends and take the kindness pledge. Challenge each other to complete as many kindness acts as possible in a single day. Visit the website to download the checklist. http://www.greatkindnesschallenge.org/.

MTV Voices. Do you like to express your opinion or hear what other people your age are saying? This no-nonsense website doesn't hold back or sugarcoat anything. This is a place where teens can discuss pop culture, everyday life, and things happening around the world. http://www .mtvvoices.com/.

My Hero. Are you interested in letting the world know about a special hero in your life? Or maybe you're looking for some inspiration? Either way, this site lets you share stories, create art, or submit a video about someone you admire. http://myhero.com/.

The 100 Day Project. Would you like to get your creative juices flowing? Commit to doing the same thing every day for one hundred days in a row. http://the100dayproject.com/.

Quibblo. Create quizzes for your friends to take, or to add to a website or blog. http://www.quibblo.com/.

Rookie. A website for teenage girls with each month's issue revolving around a particular theme. Submit content or read what others are posting. http://www.rookiemag.com/.

Scratch. Use this free website to learn computer coding. Create a game, learn animation, and share your projects with other people. https://scratch.mit.edu/.

Stage of Life. This forum allows you to share your story or read someone else's story while bringing people of different generations together to learn from each other. http://www.stageoflife.com/.

Student Voice. Do you feel like you have something to say regarding your education? Then join the #StuVoice chats every Monday night on Twitter, where students, teachers, and policy makers gather for a lively discussion. http://www.stuvoice.org/.

Teen Ink. This zine for teens allows you to publish your writing and artwork. Exchange feedback with other teens and participate in online classes. http://www.teenink.com/.

The Talent Code. Bestselling author Daniel Coyle uses sports clips and training exercises to illustrate how talent is developed. http://www.thetalentcode.com/.

Wattpad. If you have a story to tell or want to read what others are writing, then visit this site. http://www.wattpad.com/.

World Association of Young Scientists. Are you a scientist? Join this organization of youth to network, post to the forum, and exchange information with other people who share your scientific interests. http://ways.org/.

Wee World. Join 60 million users to create your own character, play games, and chat with people your own age. http://www.weeworld.com/.

Young Composers. This is a forum for youth of all ages and every musical level. Receive critiques, advice, and support from your peers and from industry professionals. http://www.youngcomposers.com/.

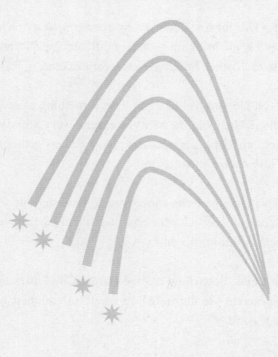

SPARK UP YOUR LEARNING

College Resources

Campus Explorer. Would you like advice on what you can do in high school to prepare for college? Visit this site for detailed information including a long list of extracurricular activities you may want to give a try. http://www.campusexplorer.com/.

College Board. Do you need help preparing for college? Would you like some online help for the SATs? If so, let this site help with the transition. https://www.collegeboard.org/.

College Insight. Compare and analyze information about college costs, size, diversity, and programs to help you narrow down your search for the perfect school. http://college-insight.org/.

College Majors 101. Not sure what you want your college major to be? That's okay because this website lets you explore all the wonderful learning opportunities available to you in college. http://www .collegemajors101.com/.

College Navigator. Find the college that is right for you by building a list of schools matching your search requirements. https://nces.ed.gov /collegenavigator.

Unigo. Get matched to the perfect college or internship with this site. Read reviews from students who are attending the school right now to see what people really think of life on campus. https://www.unigo.com/.

Uprospie. Network with students who attend the colleges you are interested in to get an inside look at campus life. https://www.uprospie.com/.

Education Resources

Edutopia. This site was created by the George Lucas Educational Foundation to promote project-based learning so students can become more engaged in the learning process. http://www.edutopia.org/.

HippoCampus. Are you having trouble with one of your homework assignments? If so, visit this site, which hosts over 5,700 videos across thirteen academic subjects. http://www.hippocampus.org/.

Khan Academy. This comprehensive instructional site provides help in math, science, technology, history, and economics through videos and activities. https://www.khanacademy.org/.

Mu Alpha Theta. This is a high school honor society for high-achieving math students. See if your school has a chapter. http://www.mualpha theta.org/.

SparkNotes. Do you need help studying for a test, writing a paper, or understanding your homework? Visit this website to get all the assistance and advice you need. http://www.sparknotes.com/.

Fellowship & Mentorship Resources

Entrepreneur. Become a student entrepreneur based on the tips and tricks on this website. http://www.entrepreneur.com/topic/young -entrepreneurs.

FIRST. Founded by Dean Kamen, who holds over four hundred patents, this organization provides mentorship to youth who are interested in science and technology. http://www.firstinspires.org/.

Inc. Get inspired while reading about other young entrepreneurs and advice they have for you. http://www.inc.com/rising-stars.

Independent Youth. Spark your creativity, network with other teens, and join a peer-mentoring program. You can also watch informational webinars and find out about local business events in your area. http://independentyouth.org/.

MDJunior. This organization pairs students up with mentors in the healthcare profession to promote education and volunteering in health-related nonprofit organizations. http://www.mdjunior.org/.

Mentor. Are you interested in finding a mentor in your area? This organization will help you find a mentoring program where you live based on your interests. http://www.mentoring.org/.

The Next Big Thing. TNBT helps youth entrepreneurs develop their business skills, obtain technology, and receive mentorship for their ideas. http://www.wearetnbt.com/.

Small Business Association. You are never too young to learn about starting a business. Learn the legal ins and outs of small business ownership. https://www.sba.gov/category/business-groups/teen.

Teen Business Forum. Start a business and network with other young entrepreneurs.http://dealbook.startl.org/company/teen-business-forum/.

Youth Citizen Entrepreneurship. Learn how to start a business from scratch, receive free training, and submit your project to a worldwide competition. https://www.entrepreneurship-campus.org.

"Money-Centsible" Resources

Fox on Stocks. Nineteen-year-old Rachel Fox gives her perspective on stock trading based on pop culture trends. http://foxonstocks.com/.

Junior Achievement. Managing your money or starting a business can be super exciting, but they require a little planning. Learn how to get started at http://www.juniorachievement.org/.

Mint. Are you saving up for something big? Whether you're saving for college, a class trip, or a car, this site will teach you how to set up a budget and reach your saving goals. https://www.mint.com/.

SimpleTuition. Compare college financial aid packages and search for scholarships. www.simpletuition.com/.

Teens Got Cents. This site proves it's never too early to start learning about finances. Follow this blog to start preparing for your financial future. http://teensgotcents.com/.

News Resources

Channel One News. Are you media savvy and like to keep up with current events? If so, visit this site daily to get your dose of the news. http://www.channelone.com.

CNN Student News. Keep up with world events and preview videos. http://www.cnn.com/studentnews.

Fanlala. Get the latest entertainment news about your favorite celebrities and musicians. https://www.fanlala.com/.

HowStuffWorks. If you have a question, this site probably has an answer. From common everyday questions to obscure information, this website will satisfy your curiosity. http://www.howstuffworks.com/.

HuffPost Teen. Get information about teens written by teen columnists. Includes advice, news, and social issues. http://www.huffingtonpost.com/teen.

Learning with the *New York Times*. Interact with content from the *New York Times* with quizzes, crossword puzzles, opinion questions, and news articles. http://learning.blogs.nytimes.com/.

TEDxTeen. Tune in to this site to watch inspirational and informative talks given by teens with amazing ideas. http://www.tedxteen.com/.

Time for Kids. Learn about real-world events and top stories. http://www.timeforkids.com/.

SPARK UP YOUR WELL-BEING
Bullying Resources

The Bully Project. This is the official website to accompany Lee Hirsch's documentary, *Bully*. This site provides movie screenings, educational tools, and opportunities for activism. http://www.thebullyproject.com/.

End to Cyber Bullying (ETCB). In eighth grade, cocreator Samuel Lam's Facebook page was spammed with negative racial comments. Instead of retreating, he's used social media to raise awareness about cyberbullying. His site provides teen counseling, information, and opportunities for teens to become activists. http://www.endcyberbullying.org/.

Pacer Center's Teens against Bullying. This site was created by teens for teens. If you or a friend are being bullied, you are not alone. Read other people's stories about being bullied, and share your own experience. Use the action plan information to develop a strategy on how you can put a stop to the bullying. http://www.pacerteensagainstbullying.org/.

Stop Bullying. This comprehensive website provides information to teens, parents, and educators about all types of bullying. http://www .stopbullying.gov/.

Health Resources

The Conscious Life. Learn the basics of how to meditate and why it is good for your spirit and your body. http://theconsciouslife.com /meditation-resources.

The Jed Foundation. This site provides information and resources to students about emotional health issues. http://www.jedfoundation.org/.

Learn to Be Healthy. Download kits with information, games, and activities on how you can lead a healthy life. http://www.learntobehealthy.org/teens.

Love Is Louder. Started by MTV and Brittany Snow to discuss issues about bullying, low self-image, loneliness, and discrimination, this site allows you to download an action kit to hold your own Love Is Louder event. http://www.loveislouder.com/.

Proud2BMe. This site and online community are written for teens by teens and focus on body image issues, confidence, and health. http://www.proud2bme.org/.

Teen Fitness Connection. With just your zip code, this site will find fitness facilities, clubs, and dance studios that offer free memberships to teens. http://www.teenfitnessconnection.org/.

WebMD for Teens. This health site answers all the questions you may have been too embarrassed to ask regarding body, health, and emotional health issues. http://teens.webmd.com/.

Yoga and Body Image. This website provides stories from different people about how yoga changes the way they view their bodies. http://www.yogaandbodyimage.com/.

Hotlines

Crisis Text Line. Text 741-741 to get support for any type of crisis.

Kids Helpline. You can web chat or email counselors about anything you want to talk about at any time of the day. http://kidshelpline.com.au/teens/.

Teen Central. Find crisis hotlines available in your state on this site. http://www.teencentral.net/Help/teenhelp.php.

Teen Line. Call, text, or email this helpline where teens offer you advice on any problem including bullying, suicide, and depression. No problem is too big or too small. https://teenlineonline.org/.

Your Life Your Voice. Text, chat, or email to get help with any type of problem. For twenty-four-hour assistance, call 1-800-448-3000. http://www.yourlifeyourvoice.org/Pages/home.aspx.

Relationships

Choose Respect. This site provides resources for teens and parents about positive relationship behaviors. http://www.chooserespect.org/.

Love Is Respect. This organization's mission is to educate and empower teens to end abusive relationships. http://www.loveisrespect.org/.

Scarleteen. This site is one of the largest resources for sexual education. It provides message boards, forums, and articles on everything having to do with your body, relationships, and sexuality. http://www.scarleteen.com/.

Sex, Etc. Get answers to your questions about sex, relationships, pregnancy, and sexual orientation at this site for teens that is authored by teens. http://sexetc.org/.

Teen Central. Do you have a question or problem and don't know who to ask to get some answers? This site will provide you with an answer within twenty-four hours. http://www.teencentral.net/.

The Trevor Project. This is the number one national organization for information on crisis intervention and resources for lesbian, gay, bisexual, and transgender youth. http://www.thetrevorproject.org/.

SPARK IT UP DISCUSSION GUIDE

R ead through this discussion guide to dig a little deeper and explore a little more broadly. Consider these questions on your own or discuss them with a friend. And remember, it's all about igniting the best parts of *you*!

1. Wooster defines *igniters* as spark lighters, and *extinguishers* as ways of thinking that disrupt potential sparks. Make a list of current extinguishers in your life and then rewrite them to represent igniters. Extinguisher: *I only have three friends at school.* Igniter: *I have three of the most loyal friends in the world.*
2. Olympic gymnast Aly Raisman says, "The bad days are what make us stronger." How can you use what you learned about failure to shift how you view setbacks? For instance, what would you do if you stumbled through a school presentation?

3. Jack Andraka was turned down by 199 labs before he found a researcher willing to help with his pancreatic cancer research. What if he had given up? What can you learn from his resilience?

4. Wooster writes, "You wouldn't tell your best pal they are fat, ugly, or weird looking." Make a list of five things you say to yourself that you'd never say to a friend.

5. One of Wooster's main arguments is that focusing on things outside yourself "makes it easier to focus on your internal self more than your external packaging." What do you think? Does participating in outside activities, helping others, or being spiritual take your attention away from how you look? In what way?

6. If you had nothing to lose and didn't fear failure, what new activities would you pursue? What possible outcomes are holding you back from trying?

7. What are some amazing things that have resulted from failure? Think about history, inventions, and professional-athlete stories.

8. Finding your passion isn't always easy. Why not make a list of problems you see and turn them into opportunities? For instance, *My school doesn't offer healthy lunch options—how I can solve this problem?*

9. During a bullying incident a passive witness stands on the sidelines, while an active witness stands up to the bully on the victim's behalf. What type of witness are you? What can you do to take a stand against bullying?

10. Youth advocate Adora Svitak tells students to become authors of their own education. What does she mean by this, and how can you implement this strategy into your own schooling?

11. Lulu Cerone created a ripple effect with her LemonAID Warrior fundraiser when it became the first of many PhilanthroParties, which led to humanitarian awards and a book deal. How can you take something you like to do and create a ripple effect? For instance, *Take online coding courses to get better at playing video*

games, which leads to doing better at a particular video game, which leads to an interest in working toward a certification in programming.

12. Identify one "marathon" (long-term) goal you'd like to pursue. Write down the steps you need to take in order to achieve this dream.

13. Define *grit*. Think of an example from the news or history where someone showed perseverance, grit, and resilience to reach their goal.

14. Think of an activity you want to try but have been too nervous to pursue. Now make a list of everything that may go wrong. Next to each item describe how you can use resilience to bounce back.

15. What was the most valuable thing you learned from *Ignite Your Spark* about yourself and the person you want to be?